This book brings to life what cyber security means to business analysts and how they should consider this topic in their work. The framework developed throughout the book is simple to understand and offers a comprehensive guide. The book contains lots of practical advice which is brought to life with relatable and enjoyable anecdotes. This is a must for any business analyst wishing to learn more and grow their understanding and appreciation of cyber security.

Victoria Banner BA, BSc, CBAP, *Business Architect, Royal London Group*

Cyber security can be a dry subject. Bindu Channaveerappa has achieved the remarkable feat of making it not only interesting but entertaining, by seeing and explaining the wider business context in her own unique style.

Nick de Voil MBCS, CITP, CBAP, CCA, *Director, De Voil Consulting,*
past president of IIBA UK, author of 'User Experience Foundations'

Cyber Security and Business Analysis is both scary and reassuring – scary because I learned so many ways that things can and do go horribly wrong, but also very reassuring in the way that Bindu provides practical ways to protect organisations through cyber security via business analysis. Reassuring too are Bindu's stories and metaphors peppered throughout the book, drawing on her deep experience and bringing light and life to what might otherwise be a challenging topic.

Dr Penny Pullan, *Editor of 'Business Analysis and Leadership' and*
Consultant at Making Projects Work Ltd

Bindu convincingly raises awareness about the pivotal role BA professionals must play in making cyber security a first-class concern. Her highly approachable book gets you started by building on what you already know and by providing the tools and stories to engage your stakeholders. I have no doubt that Bindu's book will become the de facto starting point for cyber security for many business analysis professionals.

Filip Hendrickx, *Founder and Innovating BA, altershape.eu*

A great book that truly connects the business analysis role to cyber security, the BABOK, and provides a framework and tools for business analysts to use to assess and evaluate how to ensure cyber security is part of their work and at what level.

Angela Wick, *BA-Cube Founder, LinkedIn Learning Instructor*

This is a vital primer for business analyst seeing to protect organisations from the ever-increasing risk of cyber attacks.

Kevin Brennan, *Professor at George Brown College and Business Architect*

Bindu has delivered a much-needed book that finally puts business analysts at the centre of the efforts to solve the complex cyber security challenges faced by modern enterprises.

Mark Cross, *Principal Business Analyst, Envista Consulting Ltd*

Bindu masterfully engages us with a storytelling and metaphors approach that resonates deeply, fostering significant shifts in our mindset. This book is an essential resource for integrating crucial cyber security awareness within business analysis practices. It serves as a definitive guide that can transform the situation for organisations at risk by providing the knowledge needed to address current cyber security challenges effectively.

Fabricio Laguna, *Senior Advisor for the President and CEO of the International Institute of Business Analysis*

Cyber Security and Business Analysis is an essential read for any business analyst looking to understand the often dense and seemingly uninviting world of cyber security. This book expertly demonstrates how the business analyst role can aid in the cyber security process and is often instrumental in ensuring the success of cyber security initiatives in a business. If you are just starting to work with cyber security or have been working with cyber security for years, this book will have something to offer you.

Martin Pendlebury, *Young Business Analysts*

Every piece of knowledge has to be fundamental, and that is precisely what *Cyber Security and Business Analysis* provides the reader. The cyber security framework presented in this book allows every business analyst to acquire the right security mindset and understand how security intertwines with business analysis's core concepts, knowledge areas and tasks. Practical and exceptional!

Iurii Gomon, *Founder, The Passionate Business Analyst*

I highly recommend this book to all business analysts. In particular, it frames cyber security in terms of business analysis so that as BAs we can easily and efficiently include it as part of our usual approach to requirements, discovery and elicitation, etc. Cyber security has very few champions outside of technical roles and BAs are uniquely placed to add value to this vital element of a business – this book really empowers us to be those champions.

Richard Harrison, *Principal Consultant, Herd Consulting*

Cyber Security and Business Analysis is an empowering read, packed with actionable knowledge. Whether you're a seasoned professional or simply starting your cyber security journey, this book is invaluable!

Kudzai Muchenje, *Business Analyst, SanlamAllianz*

CYBER SECURITY AND BUSINESS ANALYSIS

BCS, THE CHARTERED INSTITUTE FOR IT

BCS, The Chartered Institute for IT, is committed to making IT good for society. We use the power of our network to bring about positive, tangible change. We champion the global IT profession and the interests of individuals, engaged in that profession, for the benefit of all.

Exchanging IT expertise and knowledge
The Institute fosters links between experts from industry, academia and business to promote new thinking, education and knowledge sharing.

Supporting practitioners
Through continuing professional development and a series of respected IT qualifications, the Institute seeks to promote professional practice tuned to the demands of business. It provides practical support and information services to its members and volunteer communities around the world.

Setting standards and frameworks
The Institute collaborates with government, industry and relevant bodies to establish good working practices, codes of conduct, skills frameworks and common standards. It also offers a range of consultancy services to employers to help them adopt best practice.

Become a member
Over 70,000 people including students, teachers, professionals and practitioners enjoy the benefits of BCS membership. These include access to an international community, invitations to a roster of local and national events, career development tools and a quarterly thought-leadership magazine. Visit www.bcs.org to find out more.

Further information
BCS, The Chartered Institute for IT,
3 Newbridge Square,
Swindon, SN1 1BY, United Kingdom.
T +44 (0) 1793 417 417
(Monday to Friday, 09:00 to 17:00 UK time)
www.bcs.org/contact

http://shop.bcs.org/
publishing@bcs.uk

www.bcs.org/qualifications-and-certifications/certifications-for-professionals/

CYBER SECURITY AND BUSINESS ANALYSIS

An essential guide to secure and robust systems

Bindu Channaveerappa

Published by BCS Learning and Development Ltd, a wholly owned subsidary of BCS, The Chartered Institute for IT, 3 Newbridge Square, Swindon, SN1 1BY, UK.
www.bcs.org

Paperback ISBN: 978-1-78017-6130
PDF ISBN: 978-1-78017-6147
ePUB ISBN: 978-1-78017-6154

Ebook available

British Cataloguing in Publication Data.
A CIP catalogue record for this book is available at the British Library.

Publisher's acknowledgements
Reviewers: Martin Pendlebury and Aubrey Kudzai Muchenje
Publisher: Ian Borthwick
Commissioning editor: Heather Wood
Production manager: Florence Leroy
Project manager: Sunrise Setting Ltd
Copy-editor: The Business Blend Ltd
Proofreader: Barbara Eastman
Indexer: David Gaskell
Cover design: Alex Wright
Cover image: istock/lavin photography
Sales director: Charles Rumball
Typeset by Lapiz Digital Services, Chennai, India

To my Mum, whose dedication to learning has been a constant source of inspiration till this day. Her commitment to education has instilled in me the value of being a lifelong learner.

To my Dad, whose fearless approach to venturing into uncharted territories has taught me the importance of embracing the unknown with courage and determination.

To my four supporting pillars, Kiran, Ravi, Ronit and Rachit, whose unwavering support and encouragement have always kept me grounded and stable.

To my dear friend Terry, whose friendship and expertise have been invaluable on this journey.

CONTENTS

LIST OF FIGURES AND TABLES

AUTHOR

Bindu Channaveerappa is a business analysis consultant who is passionate about all things business analysis. Recognising the imperative need for cyber security analysis, Bindu passionately advocates for integrating cyber security into mainstream business analysis practices, and has made significant contributions to the field. She co-authored the Cybersecurity Certification (CCA) curriculum for the International Institute of Business Analysis (IIBA®) and has shaped exam questions for the CCA and Certified Business Analysis Professional (CBAP) certification, contributing to the development of IIBA standards and IIBA digital assets.

Bindu shares insights on business analysis and cyber security at international conferences and online platforms.

Along with her professional endeavours, Bindu serves as the IIBA Regional Director for Europe, the Middle East and Africa and has served the IIBA UK chapter as one of the directors. In addition, Bindu dedicates time to the Brahma Kumaris World Spiritual University, advocating for a spiritual lifestyle that fosters holistic human well-being on an international scale.

FOREWORD

The need to ensure the security of organisational assets, in particular data and other confidential information, has been a concern for many years. With the rise in online access to these assets and the increasing complexity of the technological landscape, this need has become an imperative. However, key activities such as understanding the context for cyber security, conducting detailed investigation and analysis, and determining relevant actions to address cyber security threats, are often overlooked in the pursuit of technical measures. Also, these key analysis activities require extensive knowledge and skill.

Much has been written about cyber security and the need to arm organisations against the threats posed. Too often the focus is solely on specific online threats, avoiding the broader environment and dimensions where other security threats may be exploited and where actions are also required. Leaping to protective solutions without understanding the specific organisational context and the nature of the assets that require protection, can result in actions that are irrelevant, excessive or insufficient.

Cyber Security and Business Analysis places business analysis at the heart of a successful cyber security strategy. It explains that business analysis is a key discipline in ensuring organisations are able to identify, analyse and protect against cyber security threats. The guidance provided advocates that a holistic approach is adopted and that the different types of assets, the nature of the threats posed and the required levels of security need to be aligned. Business analysts deploy an analytical mindset, focusing on understanding the root causes of concerns, questioning assumptions and uncovering detailed requirements. They understand the importance of non-functional requirements and the need to analyse them in detail, not just skimming them superficially. Without this depth, inappropriate or even inadequate security measures may be implemented and assets put at risk.

Bindu Channaveerappa has researched the cyber security arena and applied the relevant techniques and frameworks for many years and, as a practising business analyst, is only too aware how access, security and protection requirements may be overlooked or are subject to unsatisfactory analysis. In this book, she provides a wealth of frameworks, references and techniques, each of which support business analysts as they deliver one of the most vital services for their organisations. She emphasises the importance of risk assessment, and the need to avoid bias when evaluating risks, to guarantee the relevance and applicability of cyber security policies and responses. She also ensures that the people aspect is highlighted, clarifying the importance of understanding not just collaborative stakeholders but also the motivations of the cyber miscreants who are intent on damaging organisations and their assets. Critically, she identifies the financial implications of a cyber security strategy, recommending business case elements that clarify the financial implications and ensure that the case for cyber security recommendations is made.

The Business Analysis and Cyber Security Framework and the techniques shared within this book are much needed to extend the business analysis toolkit and help business analysts to ensure their organisations are provided with the most relevant advice and that organisational leaders are able to make smart decisions regarding cyber security protections. This book offers invaluable guidance for all business change and IT professionals who are working to safeguard their organisations against cyber threats, ensure the organisation's assets are protected against misuse, damage or destruction, and build secure and robust systems.

Dr Debra Paul
CEO AssistKD

ACKNOWLEDGEMENTS

This book would not have been possible without the incredible support and encouragement from many individuals and the business analysis community.

First and foremost, I would like to express my deepest gratitude to Janice McNamara who saw the potential for this book in me long before I did and planted the seed that eventually grew into this project. Your belief in me has been a guiding light and I am forever thankful for your foresight and encouragement.

I would also like to thank the dedicated reviewers who provided invaluable feedback throughout the writing process. Aubrey Kudzai Muchenje and Martin Pendlebury – your insights and suggestions were instrumental in shaping the final manuscript and I am grateful for your time and effort.

My heartfelt thanks to all who lent their voices to support this book: Adrian Reed, Angela Wick, Fabricio Laguna, Filip Hendrickx, Kevin Brennan, Aubrey Kudzai Muchenje, Iurii Gomon, Mark Cross, Martin Pendlebury, Nick de Voil, Dr Penny Pullan, Richard Harrison and Victoria Banner. Your words and support have added significant value and credibility. Debra Paul, thank you for your invaluable feedback, trust and endorsement.

A special thanks to Heather Wood for reaching out to me about writing this book when I least expected it and for her unwavering support throughout this journey. Your patience, understanding and encouragement were essential in seeing this project through to completion. I also extend my gratitude to Ian Borthwick, Florence Leroy and Sharon Nickels for their publishing expertise.

Finally, to the Brahma Kumaris Spiritual Organisation, who have been a tremendous help in my life journey, enriching it with priceless wisdom that I have gathered along the way. It is this wealth of insight and experience that I now channel into the very heart of this initiative.

Thank you all for being a part of this journey. Your encouragement and enthusiasm have been a constant source of motivation on this initiative.

ABBREVIATIONS

AI	artificial intelligence
API	application programming interface
AWS	Amazon Web Services
BABOK v3	Business Analysis Body of Knowledge (IIBA)
BACCM	Business Analysis Core Concept Model (IIBA)
BCP	business continuity plan/planning
BIA	business impact analysis
BLUF	bottom-line up front
BYOD	bring your own device
CATWOE	customer, actor, transformation, worldview, owner, environment
CD	compact disc
CDO	chief data officer
CDR	call detail record
CEO	chief executive officer
CIA Triad	confidentiality, integrity, availability
CISO	chief information security officer
CS	cyber security
DDoS	distributed denial of service
FR	functional requirement
HMRC	His Majesty's Revenue & Customs
ICO	Information Commissioner's Office
IEC	International Electrotechnical Commission
IIBA	International Institute of Business Analysis
IIoT	industrial internet of things
IoT	internet of things
IRM	Institute of Risk Management
ISMS	information security management system
ISO	International Organization for Standardization
KPI	key performance indicator
ML	machine learning

NFR	non-functional requirement
PEST	political, economic, social, technological
PESTLE	political, economic, sociological, technological, legal, environmental
PI	personal information
PIA	privacy impact assessment
PII	personally identifiable information
PMI-PBA	Project Management Institute – Professional in Business Analysis
ROI	return on investment
RPA	robotic process automation
SME	subject matter expert
SQL	structured query language
STEEPLE	social, technological, economic, environmental, political, legal, ethical
SWOT	strengths, weaknesses, opportunities, threats
UAT	user acceptance testing
VMOST	vision, mission, objectives, strategies, tactics

PREFACE

Why this book?

In today's digital age, the imperative of cyber security has never been more pronounced. With the pervasive integration of technology in every aspect of our lives, the need to safeguard sensitive information and digital assets has become paramount.

I've navigated through many projects and initiatives, each presenting its unique challenges and opportunities. Yet, it was a singular event – a cyber incident – that served as a pivotal moment in my career, catalysing a profound realisation of the critical role cyber security plays in organisational resilience and success.

Though seemingly minor at first glance, the incident revealed that the organisation was ill-prepared to confront escalating cyber threats. Despite my efforts to raise awareness and advocate for proactive cyber security measures, the gravity of the situation went largely unrecognised by senior management. It was a wake-up call, a stark reminder of the potential loss and devastation that could have ensued had the incident escalated unchecked.

Fuelled by a sense of urgency and determination, I embarked on a journey of discovery and studied security management. With this newfound knowledge, I sought to bridge the gap between traditional business analysis and cyber security. I found the role of business analysts pivotal in supporting the development and maintenance of secure and robust systems.

This newfound passion led me to collaborate as a co-author on the IIBA Cybersecurity Certification and to take this message to the business analysis communities at conferences worldwide, advocating for the holistic integration of cyber security within their analysis practices.

Yet, awareness alone was not enough. It was evident that the logical progression from awareness lay in implementation. Thus, I created a framework that business analysts could seamlessly integrate into their day-to-day practices to proactively address cyber security concerns at every stage of the business analysis life cycle. From risk assessment and mitigation to stakeholder engagement and requirements elicitation, the framework outlined herein provides a systematic approach for integrating cyber security into every facet of the business analysis process.

Recognising the inherently theoretical nature of both business analysis and cyber security, I understand the importance of presenting the content in an engaging and accessible manner. Drawing from my role as a mother, where I have frequently used stories to convey important messages to my children, I employ a similar approach throughout this book. By weaving together anecdotes, real-life incidents and relatable stories, I aim to make the content easy to grasp and memorable for you. This storytelling technique bridges the gap between abstract concepts and practical application, fostering a deeper understanding of the material presented.

As we embark on this journey together, let us recognise the imperativeness of cyber security in today's digital age and embrace our role as trusted advisors to deliver complete analysis, which includes cyber security.

Who should read this book?

This is a business analysis book for business analysts and those who perform business analysis with or without the title. The term 'business analyst' in this book refers to anyone who uses business analysis skills, tools and techniques.

A business analyst must be mindful of all the environments affecting their organisation, both the internal and external environments, along with the current and future landscapes of the business, while performing their analyses. One such aspect this book focuses on is cyber security. Cyber security was traditionally categorised as a non-functional requirement within business analysis. However, in today's business landscape, technology has become the foundation for its operation. Hence, it is essential to cover this ground to the required depth. If not, the analysis is incomplete.

A business analyst is a trusted advisor. Trust can be built and maintained only when complete truth is brought forth in the analysis, not just what the stakeholder wants to hear. As trusted advisors, business analysts must deliver a complete analysis by conducting a thorough investigation to enable informed decision-making.

Hence, it is time to shift cyber security 'left' and strategise, design, code and test it holistically at every stage of the project life cycle. And this book aims to deliver pointers to enable you to do that.

This book does not contain a definitive prescription, nor is it an academic textbook – and there cannot be one. Organisations can have numerous cyber security strategies, and they need to choose their solutions based on various parameters such as their sensitivity of data, their operations, risks, resources and so on.

Several bodies of knowledge exist within the field of business analysis, each offering unique perspectives and resources for business analysis professionals. In this book, particular emphasis is placed on two primary bodies: BCS and IIBA.

Through this book, I aim to equip you with the knowledge and tools necessary to navigate the complex landscape of cyber security, ultimately contributing to developing more secure and resilient systems. I hope you find it helpful and enjoyable and that it supports you in your day-to-day business analysis.

My best wishes,
Bindu Channaveerappa

1 THE ESSENCE OF BUSINESS ANALYSIS

Here's what you'll learn from this chapter:

- The essence of business analysis.
- Impacts of incorrect and incomplete analysis.
- Clarity on role and responsibility definitions.
- What your profession means to you.
- Perspectives on business analysis activities.
- Right place? Right reason? Right attitude?

WHAT IS BUSINESS ANALYSIS, AND WHO IS A BUSINESS ANALYST?

Although these two questions appear simple, think about them beyond their definitions. What do they mean to you at a superficial mental level and a deeper understanding level?

Addressing these two questions before diving into the content is essential and crucial to business analysts and understanding business analysis.

REFLECTION TIME

Take a moment, ponder and write down:

- What is business analysis?
- Who is a business analyst?

What is business analysis?

To grasp the essence of business analysis, let's explore it in some of its flavours from its definition to its personal significance, encompassing different perspectives and the essential mindset it demands.

Drawing from the knowledge base of the two primary bodies of knowledge, the opening chapter of Debra Paul and James Cadle's fourth edition of *Business Analysis* (2020) delves into the fundamental question of what business analysis is – a discipline dedicated to ensuring organisational changes align with business needs, which has now evolved in guiding businesses in navigating through the complexities of the change life cycle.

The International Institute of Business Analysis (IIBA) defines business analysis as: 'the practice of enabling change in an enterprise by defining needs and recommending solutions that deliver value to stakeholders'. The crux of the definition is wrapped within the phrase 'enabling change'.

A change can be enabled only when its current and future states are clearly understood.

The term 'analysis' (pl: analyses) is the process of breaking a complex topic or substance into smaller parts to understand it better (https://en.wikipedia.org/wiki/Analysis). The word comes from the Ancient Greek ἀνάλυσις (analysis, 'a breaking up' or 'an untying'; from ana 'up, throughout' and lysis 'a loosening').

Analysis – breaking complex business components into smaller parts to better understand the current state is an integral aspect of business analysis.

The inverse of analysis is synthesis. The future state can be envisioned by combining components in a different or new way to deliver the expected value.

Synthesis – putting the pieces back together again in a new or different whole is an essential aspect of business analysis.

The part of the definition of 'recommending solutions that deliver value', the expected outcome, is achieved by evaluation.

Evaluation – comparing the outcomes from breaking up and synthesis of business components by assessing their advantages and disadvantages relative to the goals and situations is a crucial aspect of business analysis.

The value proposition is to fulfil the expectations of the stakeholders by understanding their perspectives.

Perspectives – every stakeholder will have a perspective based on their organisational role, making perspectives a critical aspect of business analysis.

The four elements – analysis, synthesis, evaluation and perspectives – are foundational to understanding the core of business analysis (Figure 1.1).

Who is a business analyst?

It is apparent that a teacher teaches, a doctor helps patients heal and a bus driver drives a bus. What about a business analyst? Is it apparent what a business analyst does? When my 10-year-old asked me what I do as a business analyst, I had to stop and think.

How to make a 10-year-old understand what business analysts do? Definitions mean nothing to them, so I had to articulate in a way that is easy for a 10-year-old to understand. It was through a story. After all, stories have a timeless appeal that resonate across generations. By weaving a narrative, I could convey the essence of the role in a way that's understandable to my young audience.

Figure 1.1 Core understanding of business analysis (Copyright: I-Perceptions Consulting Ltd)

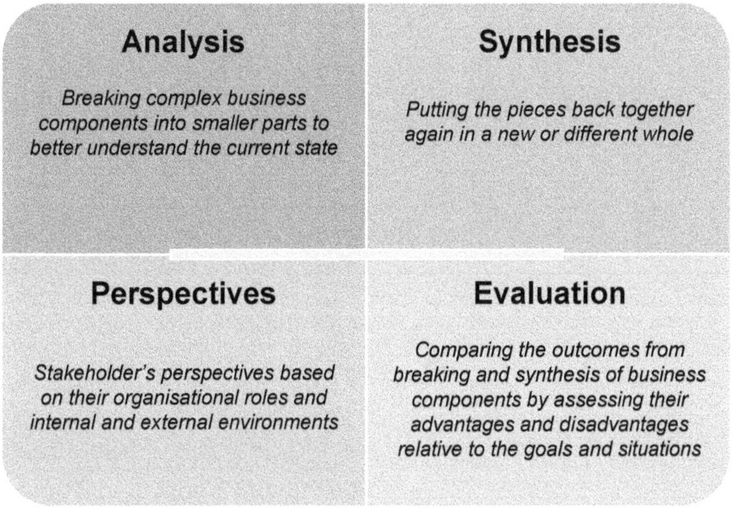

Analysis	Synthesis
Breaking complex business components into smaller parts to better understand the current state	Putting the pieces back together again in a new or different whole
Perspectives	**Evaluation**
Stakeholder's perspectives based on their organisational roles and internal and external environments	Comparing the outcomes from breaking and synthesis of business components by assessing their advantages and disadvantages relative to the goals and situations

ANALYSIS IN ACTION

Once upon a time, in a faraway land, there lived a kind and noble king. One morning a farmer came to his court with a problem that his harvest was persistently reducing year after year. He was concerned that he might not have any crop at all in the coming years and desperately needed help.

The king at once commanded one of his advisors to go and find out more about the problem and present the findings to solve the farmer's problem.

The advisor accompanied the farmer home to understand the situation and the problem in every detail. He asked the farmer several questions, such as:

- When did the farmer first notice the reduction in the harvest?
- What was the impact of this situation on his livelihood?
- Were there any other farmers who had the same problem?
- What remedies had they already tried?

The advisor then walked around the farm, checking the crop, the soil and the water in the well. He also conversed with the farm workers, attentively listening and making notes. He met with the neighbouring farmers to check if they had a similar problem and to learn what they did to solve it. He undertook the research for several days, consulted a few experts as required and collated all the information. Finally, he completed his investigation, identified the root cause of the problem and documented the findings. The analysis was complete, and he formulated proposals for a few solution options based on the results.

Solution options

The underlying reason for the reduction in the crop was due to reduced water level and the soil drying. As a result, the yield was not being supplied with sufficient water. This situation persisted, drying the ground year after year. The advisor devised several solutions by collaborating with the experts to address the root cause of the problem and its effects.

The first solution option was a quick, temporary fix that required the least investment of resources. It was to dig the well even deeper to obtain more water. However, there was a risk in this option. The neighbouring farmers had already tried this solution, and the results were inconsistent. Only a few wells replenished the water, and others didn't. Therefore, this option could not guarantee to solve the problem and produce the desired outcome, but this risk was acceptable.

The second solution option was to set up a mechanical infrastructure to pump water from the nearby lake into the farm. This option required more investment than the first and was not a quick fix. Due to the higher cost of setting up the infrastructure, this second option could be extended to the neighbouring farmers dealing with a similar situation, thereby sharing the installation and ongoing maintenance costs. However, this solution was also not a permanent fix and could not guarantee the desired outcome. Due to the drying up of the soil, the water levels in the lake, too, could further reduce over time. Additionally, the lake was a reservoir, and using the water immediately could create a deficit during droughts, giving rise to another crisis. Therefore, the current water usage in the lake would not be dependable, making this a high-risk option.

The third solution option was a longer-term, efficient and permanent solution. It was to plant more trees around the farming land that would hold water and avoid drying up the soil in the future. This option could improve the soil quality and rejuvenate the wells and the other water bodies. It addressed the current problem and would enhance the harvests' quality and quantity.

The advisor submitted this report to the king. Then, with all the findings and the solution options, the king could decide on the best solution for the farmer's problem.

I told my son that, in this day and age, business analysts are like this advisor. They analyse the problem, research all the relevant facts, communicate and collaborate with the concerned teams, identify the root cause of the situation and propose solution options.

As I said this, my son immediately remarked that a business analyst solves people's problems, and that statement nailed it.

In essence, business analysts are problem solvers. They tease out the problem situation to find suitable solutions to solve the problem. However, in this process, can a business analyst:

- Miss out on analysing relevant pieces of information?
- Ignore seeing the different perspectives?
- Perform inadequate research?

How would any of the above shortcomings affect the analysis and the findings? And why is it so important that a business analyst delivers a complete and correct analysis?

IMPACTS OF INCORRECT AND INCOMPLETE ANALYSIS

Let's consider a few scenarios to illustrate the consequences of inaccurate and incomplete analysis in the above story. These scenarios demonstrate how flawed solutions can exacerbate existing problems or introduce new issues and risks.

Scenario 1

The problem is deteriorating harvest.

Analysis

Assuming the perceived problem as the real problem.

Potential solution option

Import crops or alternate food supplies from neighbouring states or countries.

Impacts

- How sustainable is it to import food supplies from neighbouring states or countries?
- What will be the process requirements? Will it be simple or complicated?
- Will the imported crop be the same or different?
- If different, can the people accept the new diet?
- Are there any side effects from the new diet we must prepare for?
- What are the requirements for the new type of crop in terms of storage, climate, etc.?

Outcome

The perceived problem is being addressed rather than the root cause.

Although this solution may solve the problem temporarily, it will only perpetuate more problems, incurring unnecessary investments, effort, money, resources, time and so on, and ultimately, it fails to address the underlying root cause of the situation.

Scenario 2

A new fancy machine will solve the problem and is the talk of the town. Everyone is raving about the new fancy machine easing farmers' efforts.

Analysis

Assuming the efficacy of the fancy machine has been tested and verified to ease farmers' lives, as everyone has the same understanding, including the farmers, workers, neighbouring villagers and the research data.

Potential solution option

Install the new fancy machine as quickly as possible to avoid missing the window for the forthcoming harvest.

Impacts

- It is reported that the machine requires regular maintenance for water leaks, which is expensive, and therefore:
  - How will the farmers afford the expensive maintenance cost?
  - How long will this be sustainable?
  - Why was this not discussed with the farmers earlier?
- Farmers must undergo mandatory training to learn about machine technology, operations and maintenance, so dedicated time for this activity must be set aside.
  - Can the farmers allocate additional time for training?
  - If not, what will be the alternative?
  - Who else can operate the machine to avoid downtime?
- The machine requires a customised infrastructure to secure the equipment and its usage.
  - Has the feasibility of the infrastructure been assessed?
  - If not, who is responsible for ensuring the machine's security requirements?
  - Without proper security measures in place, anyone could gain access to the machine room and tamper with the equipment, potentially causing damage, even if it's accidental.
  - Farm animals could also enter the machine room and damage the machine.
  - Some farm workers who have a personal feud with the farmer could damage the machine intentionally.

Outcome

Due to incomplete analysis, the required due diligence for the machine's security, implementation and usage is not ensured. As a result, the solution to install the new fancy machine to ease farmers' lives fails, and once again the root cause remains unresolved.

The scenarios presented above provide valuable opportunities for introspection, encouraging us to revisit our past projects or situations where desired outcomes weren't met. It prompts us to consider what factors might have led to this shortfall. Did we accept the problem at face value without delving deeper into its underlying causes? Was there an assumption that someone else bore the responsibility? Reflecting on these questions offers insights into areas for improvement and enables us to refine our problem-solving approaches for the future.

A business analyst is responsible for delivering a complete analysis to resolve the problem successfully.

REFLECTION TIME

Take a moment, ponder and write down:

- What were the reasons and assumptions that may have contributed to falling short or led to not achieving the desired end goal in any of your projects?

CLARITY ON ROLE AND RESPONSIBILITY DEFINITIONS

Continuing to explore the essence of business analysis further, it is essential to explore the definitions of role and responsibility in an organisational context. There are several titles for business analyst roles and the responsibilities vary within those roles, just like no two projects are usually the same or similar, even within the same domain or organisation.

A role is essentially a label assigned to a position, outlining a set of expected activities. On the other hand, responsibility entails taking ownership of executing those activities successfully, meeting expectations. While a role is more of a static designation, responsibility is dynamic, an experience of fulfilling those duties successfully. The manifestation of a role relies solely on action, and it's the execution of these actions that defines one's responsibility.

It is imperative to understand this distinction because business analysis is a responsibility. It requires all human faculties to be involved. It is not a monotonous and mundane activity, but a conscious undertaking. One has to bring physical, mental and emotional faculties to perform business analysis to deliver a complete analysis. Every business analyst must have this clarity regardless of their role and title.

WHAT DOES YOUR PROFESSION MEAN TO YOU?

What I have found for myself is that business analysis is more than a definition. Along with the acquired skills, techniques and tools from a business analyst toolkit to solve a problem, I reflect on the problem that I am addressing, and most times I have found the solution options emerging from within.

A role can be manifested only through action. And how that action is performed determines 'responsibility'.

Along with the tangible work that business analysts deliver, I find this profession teases one's curiosity and the desire to learn something new on every project. The new learning and experience bring inner satisfaction for the change made towards something new and creating a positive impact towards the end goal.

In her Facebook post 'Hobby, Job, Career, Vocation', Elizabeth Gilbert brings clarity to these four terms, which are often used interchangeably with different connotations. They are four different words and mean four different things (Gilbert, 2016).

On hobby

A hobby is something that is done for pleasure. The most important thing is that the stakes with a hobby are low, and the hobby rarely affects those around the individual. It's just done for the joy of that thing. It's not required, but nice to have.

On job

According to Elizabeth, at least for most people, you must have a job to pay the bills in the materialistic world. The great thing about a job is that it doesn't have to be excellent. It doesn't have to fulfil you. It doesn't have to be joyful. It just has to pay. It is the exchange of your services for money.

On career

Elizabeth explains that a career is a job you are passionate about and love. A career is something you are willing to make sacrifices for. You are willing to work extra hours. You are willing to put your life on hold for this thing because you believe in the mission of your career. You should love your career or not have one.

On vocation

She elaborates on vocation as a calling, a divine invitation. A vocation is the voice of the universe in your ear saying, 'We want you to do this thing, use your talents and gifts and make this thing.'

She further cites that the term vocation originates from Latin – a calling to be called. A vocation is the highest possible pursuit you can do. A career could end, but a vocation need not. So what does business analysis mean to you?

REFLECTION TIME

Take a moment, ponder and write down:

- What is business analysis for you? Is it a job, career or vocation?
- Is it a conscious, informed decision to be an analyst?
- Why do you want to be an analyst?

PERSPECTIVES ON BUSINESS ANALYSIS ACTIVITIES

Delving deeper into unravelling the essence of business analysis, cultivating the right perspective and attitude is absolutely paramount. Do you know the story of the three bricklayers?

In his book, *What Can A Man Believe?*, Bruce Barton (1927), cites this story. After the great fire set London ablaze, the world-famous architect Christopher Wren was commissioned to rebuild St Paul's cathedral. The parable states that Christopher witnessed three bricklayers with three different attitudes while building the cathedral.

He went to the first bricklayer and asked: 'What are you doing?' The bricklayer grumpily responded: 'I am a bricklayer. I lay bricks, working hard to feed my family.'

He then went to the second bricklayer and asked the same question. The second bricklayer answered: 'I am a builder. I am building a wall.'

When the same question was put to the third bricklayer, he beamed with a big smile and passion for what he was doing. He enthusiastically replied: 'I am a cathedral builder. I am helping Christopher Wren to build this great cathedral.'

The same activity but whole different mindsets. The perspectives in this parable are insightful to everyone, especially business analysts. Business analysts cannot perform like the first or the second bricklayer. The work demands them to be no less than the third bricklayer.

RIGHT PLACE? RIGHT REASON? RIGHT ATTITUDE?

Are you in the right place, for the right reasons and with the right attitude. I have asked several people from generations different from my own about their reason for choosing their careers. In most cases, I received a similar response: to support their family, build their dream, buy their expensive toy and so on. Only a few responded for the love of that work.

That handful of people chose their profession out of sheer passion for the work, driven by the desire to make a difference. While we all have personal lives to nurture, dreams to pursue and joys to relish without guilt, it's essential to ensure that the work occupying most of our day receives the attention it warrants. Neglecting this can compromise the quality of our output. Regardless of the nature of one's job, clarity regarding the responsibilities attached to it is vital for successful execution, just like the third bricklayer.

Now, whether you've deliberately pursued the path of a business analyst or stumbled into the role by chance, it's crucial to reflect on your journey. Regardless of how you arrived here, dedicating your full attention to the role is paramount.

There exists an undocumented trust between a doctor and their patient, as well as an undocumented faith in the doctor's diagnosis. Similarly, between a business analyst and their client, there's an unspoken trust in the analysis to furnish all essential facts and perspectives, facilitating stakeholders to make informed decisions. This trust can only be established and upheld through consistently delivering comprehensive analyses. Consequently, business analysts emerge as trusted advisors for their clients.

There is an undocumented trust between a business analyst and their client to deliver a complete analysis to enable informed decision-making.

Concluding the first chapter, I am leaving with you a question to ponder: as a trusted advisor, can a business analyst exclude cyber security from their analysis, with the assumption that the technical or cyber security teams are responsible for all cyber-security-related requirements? No, the non-functional requirements do not cover all cyber security requirements, and we'll see why in the next chapter.

TAKEAWAY QUESTIONS

- What are your key learning points in this chapter?
- What is the one lesson that you will implement?
- How do you summarise your perspectives on business analysis?

2 BEGINNING OF THE CYBER SECURITY SAGA

Here's what you'll learn from this chapter:

- What cyber security means to you.
- How real this is.
- Taking a step back to gain perspective.
- What game they are playing.
- Cyber security is about more than just IT.
- Expansion is the future.
- What business analysts can do.

WHAT DOES CYBER SECURITY MEAN TO YOU?

What comes to your mind when you see or hear the word cyber security? For example, a compliance team member might say 'it's about the compliance of cyber security laws, like privacy'; somebody working in an IT team might say 'it's about securing the network or firewalls'; a system architect may say 'it's about securing the data and systems'; and most business teams would say 'it's technical in nature, and hence the IT or the cyber security team is responsible'. If you were a business analyst, what would you say? No, it's not just a part of or limited to non-functional requirements. What comes to your mind when you see or hear the word cyber security?

REFLECTION TIME

Before you continue reading further, take a moment to ponder:

- What does cyber security mean to you?

Backstory

A few years back, I would have said the same as the business teams: cyber security is the responsibility of the IT or the security teams, and I do not have to bother about it.

Security was limited to non-functional requirements (NFRs) – e.g. who needs to access the system and at what levels – until a personal experience fundamentally changed my perspective on cyber security.

I was working on a customer subscription product, and the data available for the subscription were the organisation's intellectual property. I was assigned to work on an enhancement that was at the bottom of the team's backlog. Note that the change was not seen as a business priority, which is why it was at the bottom of the backlog.

It was brought to my attention that the business and technical teams had already devised a solution for that problem, but it was not yet implemented because there were other items on the backlog that had a higher priority. As a diligent business analyst, I delved into the problem to assess if the initial solution was still viable. This involved understanding the root cause, which prompted discussions with the business, development and operations teams. To my dismay, the analysis revealed a shocking truth: the root cause of the problem was a recurring data breach, which had gone unnoticed despite multiple occurrences. Operational reports showed discrepancies attributed to heavy data downloads, yet no action had been taken.

Contemplating the potential ramifications, I couldn't help but imagine the catastrophic impact if all the data had been freely available on the internet. Not only would it have compromised the organisation's customers, but it also posed a grave threat to the organisation's reputation. Such a breach could even have endangered the organisation's very existence.

This revelation underscored the criticality of the issue, which the organisation had categorised as a low-priority and low-risk backlog item. It was this realisation that ignited my journey to delve deeper into cyber security.

HOW REAL IS THIS?

Cyber attacks were the fifth top-rated risk in 2020 across public and private sectors, globally increased by 125% in 2021, compared to 2020, and continue to be on the rise. From internet of things (IoT) cyber attacks alone, the number of attacks is expected to double by 2025 (AAG, 2024). Additionally, World Economic Forum's 2020 Global Risk Report states that the rate of detection (or prosecution) was as low as 0.05 per cent in the USA (McLean, 2024).

Let me share another couple of high-profile incidents to gain a deeper perspective.

HMRC

One notable incident reportedly took place in HMRC's Child Benefit department in 2007. It was reported that all the child benefit data (including personal details of the children who were getting the benefit and their parents' personal and bank details) were copied onto password-protected but unencrypted compact discs (CDs) and posted to the National Audit Office through an unsecured and untracked channel (BBC, 2007). Some say that the CDs reached their destination, and some say they were lost in transit, but nobody knows for sure. There are different versions of this incident, but I want to bring your attention to some potential causes for this breach:

- Failure to separate the crucial/sensitive data.
- Failure to encrypt the data.
- Failure for not conveying the data in a secure and trackable way.
- Failure to have an appropriate process for handling these data.

Reports from the time suggest that the person who copied the data and posted the CDs was unaware of the risks and was only following the instructions given by their seniors. This incident took place in 2007, and clearly we don't use CDs to transfer data anymore. We have made a lot of progress in terms of technology and ring-fenced data with legal regulations, yet this problem continues to rise. Have we made any progress in the true sense? Let's look at the second incident that occurred nearly a decade later.

TalkTalk

TalkTalk is an internet data provider. In 2009, TalkTalk acquired another company called Tiscali. As part of the acquisition, it appears that, along with the systems, Tiscali's system vulnerabilities were onboarded too. Later, in 2015, TalkTalk's database was compromised multiple times, and customers' personal and financial data were exposed (BBC).

In essence, TalkTalk suffered a significant and sustained cyber attack, and apparently only responded when it received an email demanding ransom. It is said that they didn't monitor their internal operational reports, which were apparently showing discrepancies. In the beginning, TalkTalk suspected that up to four million customers' data were compromised, and reports from the time suggest that it took several months for TalkTalk to understand the magnitude of the breach. Later on, the Information Commissioner's Office (ICO) confirmed that the attack saw the personal details of 156,959 customers accessed, including the bank account number and sort code of 15,656 customers. As a result, TalkTalk incurred damages of up to £40 million, lost 101,000 customers and the ICO imposed a £400,000 fine. The shocking fact was that the Metropolitan Police confirmed the arrest of a teenager and a 20-year-old in connection with this breach. Once again, here I would like to bring your attention to the following potential causes for the failure:

- Failure to remove the vulnerable webpages.
- Failure to update a patch that apparently was available three-and-a-half years before the attack.
- Failure to undertake proactive monitoring activities to discover vulnerabilities.
- Failure to implement the defence for a common type of attack.

Like HMRC and TalkTalk, many more reputable organisations have become the victims of cyber security breaches. They had security frameworks implemented or accredited to one or other security standards. They had their legal and regulatory teams who complied with the laws. They had a dedicated cyber security team in place and, despite all boxes ticked, they were not secured.

Research has repeatedly shown that most cyber security incidents are due to a lack of awareness, and hence 'people' are the weakest link. The above incidents reinforce too that the underlying cause is the lack of awareness.

Why is this the case? What are we missing here?

TAKING A STEP BACK TO GAIN PERSPECTIVE

Let's take a step back to gain perspective on the root causes of this mammoth issue affecting everyone professionally and personally. Gaining a perspective on the background will help us to evaluate why a focus change towards cyber security is necessary.

I started my career as a consultant analyst developer during the late 1990s. My job was to work with clients, understand their business requirements, design a database, build a system to meet their business needs, prepare manuals and train users to use the new application. I was doing all of these things on a standalone computer. All my code, executables, operating system and database, including the customer data, were in one physical system.

Figure 2.1 Technology expansion (Copyright: I-Perceptions Consulting Ltd)

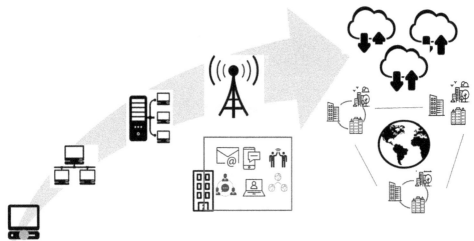

The only vulnerability apart from securing the physical equipment was using a floppy disk, which was used to copy data in and out of the computer and could potentially corrupt the files if it contained a virus. Even if a virus corrupted a file, anti-virus software was available that could clean the data. This solution could be replicated on any other infected computers within the organisation. A single solution worked for all computers.

Later, computers were connected as clients to servers, creating local and wide area networks. Today with the advent of the internet and other technological advancements, systems are distributed across the globe (Figure 2.1). For instance, customers can initiate a transaction in one location on a device and complete the same transaction in another place and at a different time.

Across the spectrum of change

Technology has advanced from wired to wireless to wearable. It is conceivable that technology may be implantable in the future. Imagine the potential weaknesses or vulnerabilities in a globally distributed system. What can go wrong in this new landscape? The list of potential vulnerabilities is seemingly endless.

Disrupting and challenging the status quo and using technology creatively within the business ecosystem has become the default way of thinking for innovative organisations. In recent years, user experience enhancements have been made by pushing out system boundaries, making imagination the new boundary. The more technology expands, the more vulnerable the ecosystem gets, and the more security controls are required.

> The more technology expands, the more vulnerable the ecosystem gets, and the more security controls are required.

In a truly interconnected world, there is no one solution to this cyber security challenge. Unlike the times when information was passed between systems by floppy disks and dial-up modems, vulnerabilities in this new landscape come with their own risks and impacts. There are additional legal and compliance requirements to adhere to, requiring different defence solutions, which could be technical and non-technical. Solutions now involve people management, process management, disaster recovery, business continuity and more.

Throughout my journey as a business analyst, I've adapted to the progressing technology and changing business needs. As the businesses started to expand, a list of user or system requirements back then began to develop into NFRs and functional requirements (FRs). Historically, security was considered a type of NFR, usually restricted to roles and permissions. With the changing business and technology landscape and increased cyber security threats, this view on security is no longer sufficient.

> When we pick up one end of the stick, we also pick up the other.
>
> Along with technology comes cyber security.

Today, robotics and artificial intelligence (AI) have become part of many people's lives, with robotic dogs patrolling the parks or Alexa and Eilik (a mini-robot) on our desktops or as personal assistants for home. This is the beauty of technology. However, as the saying goes, when we pick up one end of the stick, we also pick up the other. Along with technology comes cyber security. The obvious question that arises is why organisations are missing this.

WHAT GAME ARE THEY PLAYING?

Simon Sinek, an author and motivational speaker, talks in his book, *The Infinite Game* (2019), about the finite and infinite games organisations play knowingly or unknowingly.

Finite game

A finite game is one where there will be known players, fixed rules and an agreed objective, where there is a set goal to achieve and, in the end, there will be winners and losers. This equation works just fine when there are at least two finite players.

Infinite game

In an infinite game, there'll be unknown players, and the rules are changeable. The objective is to keep the game going, i.e. play to perpetuate the game. If one is tired of playing or wants to get out, they can, and another person will take over, continuing the game. This equation also works fine when there are two 'infinite' players.

Problems arise when you put a finite player versus an infinite player because the finite player is playing to win, and the infinite player is playing to stay in the game. As a result, the finite player will get frustrated and find themselves in crisis.

It's the same in the game of business. By its very definition, the game of business is an infinite game. However, organisations play it as a finite game. 'They don't even know the game they're in', says Simon (2019).

Every organisation aspires to be the best, but the question remains: best in what? Are their metrics clearly defined? Even if they are, they often revolve around competition, perpetually striving to outdo rivals. This can be seen where organisations just want to launch a product or service or secure prestigious awards for being the best organisation.

Simon continues to note that one can't make strategic decisions by studying the competition. One can only make tactical decisions by studying the competition.

Organisations need to understand that they're playing to stay in the game, and this understanding radically changes the kinds of decisions they make.

The infinite player understands that sometimes you are ahead and sometimes behind. Sometimes your product is better, and sometimes it's not. The goal isn't to be the best every day. The goal isn't to outdo your competition every day. The goal should be to stay in the game and experience the journey of playing and staying in the game.

Being an infinite player, an organisation should focus on creating robust products by closing all the security loopholes and delivering better value to end users. That will keep the organisation going in the long run.

A finite player is playing to win, and an infinite player is playing to stay in the game.

Being an infinite player, an organisation should focus on improving its product, closing all the security loopholes, making them robust and delivering better value to end users. That will keep the organisation going in the long run.

CYBER SECURITY IS MORE THAN JUST IT

Organisations are focusing on just putting their products out and capitalising on the quick wins, which is a finite game, and so each product has a short and finite life span.

Many products are out in the market with vulnerabilities – from light bulbs, security cameras, fish tanks, kettles and thermostats to healthcare products. Ransom attacks on hospitals have increased to 123 per cent and nearly $21 billion in ransomware cost, according to the Cynerio research report (Lauver, 2022), which examine the current outlook of connected medical device security in hospitals. A ransomware attack caused disruptions in a hospital that led to a newborn's death (Zacharakos, 2023).

Choosing victory or fulfilment, winning the war or losing the battle, being a finite player or enjoying the process as an infinite player is a constant battle. It becomes an accepted practice to lean towards instant gratification or take a shortcut for a quick win within organisations and society, but in reality, life is a marathon and not a sprint.

EXPANSION IS THE FUTURE

Research from Gartner brought forth four emerging technologies and trends for 2023. Two of the four concern cyber security. The 'smart world' – a fusion of physical and digital experiences – and the 'transparency and privacy' of personal data collection (Nguyen, 2023).

McKinsey Digital state that advances in AI, machine learning, robotics and other technologies have increased the pace of change tenfold, and they estimate that 50 billion devices will be connected to the industrial internet of things (IIoT) by 2025. They highlight that tech literacy becomes core to every role, and businesses need to be ready to cope with the pace and proliferation of technological innovations (Van Kuiken, 2022).

Cyber security is everyone's responsibility. Yet, as has often been said, 'everyone's responsibility is nobody's responsibility'.

WHAT CAN BUSINESS ANALYSTS DO?

What can (or should) business analysts do? Or does the problem exceed the scope of business analysis? The key question is: Who is responsible for cyber security? A tricky one to answer.

Imagine a customer walking into a shop, accidentally falling due to a slippery surface or stumbling due to an obstruction. In this situation, who do you think is responsible for the accident? Is it the cleaner, staff, security guard, store manager, senior management, etc.? Who in your home is responsible for securing the doors, windows or valuables? Now that you have gained a broader perspective on the topic, take a moment to ponder this question. Who is responsible for cyber security? The answer, perhaps, is that everyone has a responsibility towards cyber security. Yet, as has often been said, 'everyone's responsibility is nobody's responsibility'.

Business analysts are well-placed to pick up the baton, step up to ask difficult yet crucial questions and ensure that cyber security is kept firmly in the spotlight. Chapter 1 highlighted the responsibilities that come with the role of a business analyst in co-creating the value chain, and protection of that value chain is an intrinsic part of the responsibility.

Before we address the question of what business analysts can do, it is imperative to understand the difference between the role of a business analyst and the role of a cyber security analyst. They both are at different ends of a spectrum (Figure 2.2). They both perform analysis, but play in different playgrounds. Business analysts focus on the value proposition, and cyber security analysts focus on securing everything relating to IT and cyberspace.

Figure 2.2 Analysts spectrum (Copyright: I-Perceptions Consulting Ltd)

Business analysts need not be cyber security experts, but instead extend the scope of their analysis to include security holistically. They can collaborate with cyber security specialists as needed for each project, much like they consult with business subject matter experts (SMEs) to gain deeper insights into the business. And to do that, they need to have the required foundational knowledge to identify the security requirements across the project delivery and reach out to the SMEs accordingly (Figure 2.3).

It is well-established that security cannot be an afterthought or a patch at the end of the project and must be baked into the solution, starting from project inception (Figure 2.4).

Figure 2.3 Overview of cyber security knowledge for business analysts (Copyright: I-Perceptions Consulting Ltd)

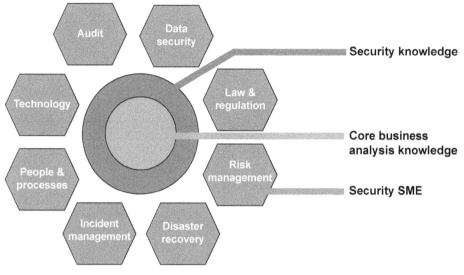

Figure 2.4 Holistic analysis (Copyright: I-Perceptions Consulting Ltd)

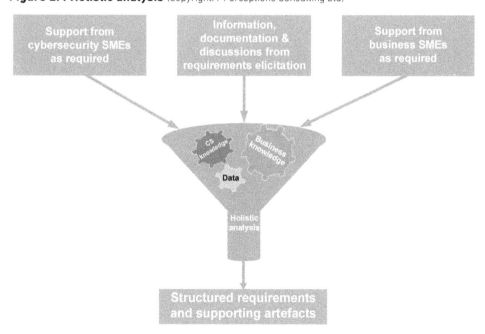

TAKEAWAY QUESTIONS

- What are your key learning points in this chapter?
- What is the one lesson that you'll implement?
- How do you summarise your perspectives on cyber security?

3 THE AWAKENING JOURNEY STARTS HERE

Here's what you'll learn from this chapter:

- Definition of cyber security.
- Introduction to the Business Analysis and Cyber Security Framework.
- How to approach security.
- Security objectives – the CIA Triad.
- Security violations.
- Additional security goals.
- Business benefits and impacts – two sides of the same coin.

WHAT IS CYBER?

The term 'cyber' is commonly used to refer to the internet, digital or the virtual world and is suffixed with anything related to the internet, digital or the virtual world. The term originated from the Greek word '*kybereo*', which means to guide, steer or control. It gained popularity in 1948 when the American mathematician Norbert Wiener coined 'cybernetics' – the scientific study of controlling and communicating with systems using technology (Dawkins, 2022). From this term emerged a series of derivatives to describe everything related to the internet, such as cyber security, cyberspace, cybercrime, etc.

WHAT IS SECURITY?

The National Institute of Standards and Technology defines security as 'the state of being free from danger or threat' (https://csrc.nist.gov/glossary). A 'thing' can be in danger or have a threat only if it is valuable or of great worth to someone at that given time. Therefore, security is equal to the protection provided to a valued possession against all its threats.

Security = Protection of Value against the Threats

In this equation, 'Security' is equated to the **action** of 'Protection' **applied** to 'Value' in the **presence** of 'Danger' or 'Threat'. This equation highlights two profound insights:

1. An **action** is to be taken to protect something of value. Systems or processes do not defend themselves, and action must be taken to protect them.
2. That action can only be taken when the dangers or threats are **recognised**. We cannot protect something when we do not know the dangers or threats against it.

Security = Protection of Value against the Threats

THE BUSINESS ANALYSIS AND CYBER SECURITY FRAMEWORK

To effectively apply this formula, a structured and systematic approach for identifying risks, threats and vulnerabilities throughout each stage of the project life cycle is fundamental. Along with the cyber security knowledge provided within this book, business analysts will need a framework to seamlessly integrate cyber security analysis into their day-to-day business analysis activities while navigating the project life stages.

The Business Analysis and Cyber Security Framework (© 2024 I-Perceptions Consulting Ltd) enables business analysts to holistically extend their analysis to include cyber security aspects across the project development phases. This chapter lays the groundwork for the framework's development and establishing essential principles, and subsequent chapters will progressively elaborate on this framework, incorporating both business analysis and cyber security elements.

Mindset is the first building block of the framework, the foundation of the framework. A mindset is a mental attitude or perspective based on one's belief systems, which is the amalgamation of one's upbringing and environment. While Chapter 1 delved into business analysis perspectives and mindset, this chapter establishes the groundwork for embracing the security mindset.

What does security mindset mean?

A **security mindset** is having an additional lens to perceive everything from a security viewpoint, a heightened awareness to see the value of the asset, its threats and the required protection. As with common sense being one of the basic constructs within the realm of consciousness yet a rare commodity, so the security mindset is a critical aspect of security that can be easily missed. A security mindset is like any other muscle that needs to be developed and regularly maintained.

A mindset is a mental attitude or perspective based on one's belief systems, which is the amalgamation of one's upbringing and environment.

A security mindset is having an additional lens to perceive everything from a security viewpoint, a heightened awareness to see the value of the asset, its threats and the required protection.

Let's look at an example to understand this better. If I were to ask you how you would secure your bike, you might probably say it would be like the first image in Figure 3.1, and may also say that this is how everyone locks their bikes. However, if I ask you if the bike is protected, we know the obvious. This is the difference between doing things without and with a security mindset.

Figure 3.1 Bike parked and stolen (Copyright: I-Perceptions Consulting Ltd)

Similarly, many reputable organisations have become the victims of cyber security breaches. They had ticked all the security obligations; they had security frameworks implemented or accredited to one or other security standards; they had their legal and regulatory teams who complied with the laws; they had a dedicated cyber security team in place – yet, despite all the boxes ticked, they were not secured. A security mindset proves that security is much more than just implementing controls. Research proves that most cyber security incidents are due to people and process vulnerabilities, leading to the root cause of not being aware of the security mindset.

As the saying goes, the centre of a storm is often the calmest spot. Similarly, for business analysts, embracing both the business analysis mindset (discussed in Chapter 1) and the security mindset is akin to finding that tranquil center. It provides them with clarity on what requires safeguarding and the level of security it necessitates.

REFLECTION TIME

Take a moment, ponder and write down:

- Can you identify something that is of value? An asset being secured without a security mindset? Now, with the shift in your understanding, how would you approach securing that asset?

My recommendation is to reflect on a personal and an organisation asset, as it helps strengthen the security mindset. Do not skip this exercise as the more you engage it, the more robust your mindset becomes.

DEFINITION OF CYBER SECURITY

To understand the definition of cyber security, let's first understand the different avatars (as I call it) that cyber security projects manifest. As business or system analysts, we will have worked on security projects but without a security mindset.

Many of us have experience working on projects involving the implementation of technical or process controls, such as user authentication through passwords for accessing products or applications, the enforcement of multi-layered authorisations for critical functionalities, or the maintenance of role-based access to processes and systems. However, it's essential to reflect: was there a comprehensive grasp of the security requirements or was role-based access merely regarded as another feature the product offered, like the bike analogy mentioned earlier?

Was there a clear alignment with the security objectives outlined in your organisation's security policy regarding activities such as encrypting personally identifiable information (PII) data, securing networks and firewalls, establishing secure communication channels between gateways, or engaging in compliance projects to meet legal and regulatory obligations regarding data security? Or did the implementation lack cohesion with these objectives, assuming that the security and IT teams will ensure this alignment (Figure 3.2)?

Figure 3.2 Cyber security activities (Copyright: I-Perceptions Consulting Ltd)

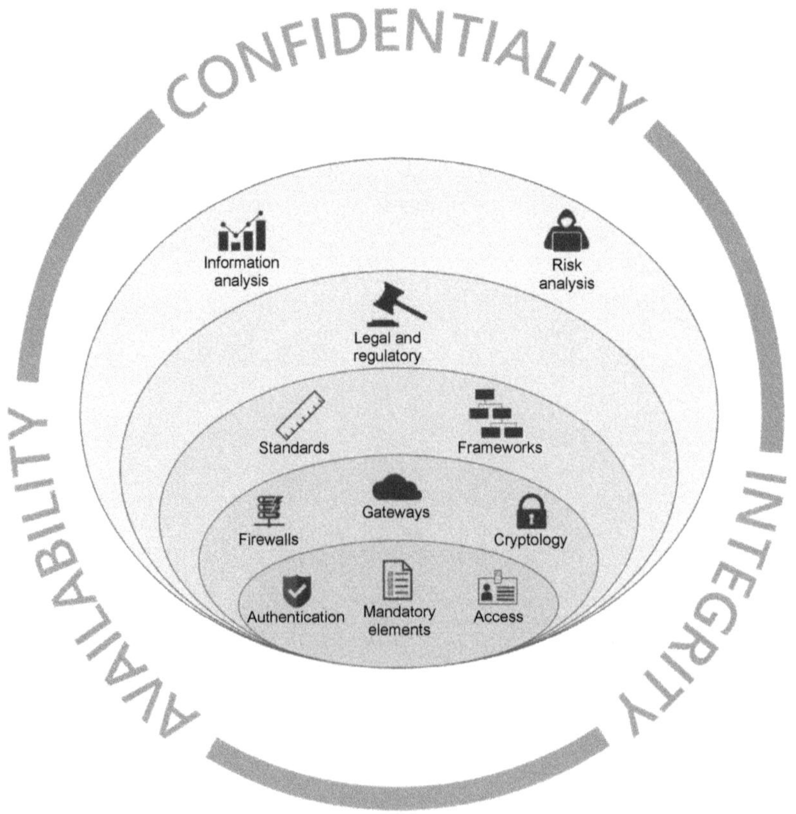

Were we truly aware of what we were protecting or did it merely seem like another project task? When faced with legal compliance obligations, did we invest the necessary effort to fully grasp the underlying rationale or did compliance become just another checkbox to tick off? Moreover, why do certain data sets hold more significance than others and what drives organisations' varying needs for data purging? These inquiries prompt reflection within the organisational context, urging us to comprehend the journey of information assets as they traverse through various systems and processes, undergoing transformation along the way.

Only with a holistic view will we be able to summarise the definition of cyber security, which is 'the protection of systems, networks, applications, processes, people-systems interactions and data within the cyberspace' (CISCO, 2024).

> Cyber security is the protection of systems, networks, applications, processes, people–systems interactions and data within the cyberspace.

HOW TO APPROACH SECURITY

There are two approaches to achieving security (Figure 3.3), although both achieve the same goal of protecting an asset but from two opposite perspectives.

Figure 3.3 Security approaches (Copyright: I-Perceptions Consulting Ltd)

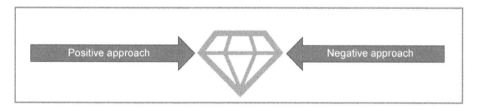

The positive approach, also known as the preventive or objective-based approach, is the ability to proactively resist or eliminate threats to an asset. This objective-based (protecting the asset) approach is where an asset is protected because of its value and the objectives identified to preserve its integrity, such as role-based access control to sensitive information and systems, authentication and authorisations. It is, therefore, the maintenance of the identified objectives for an asset.

The negative approach, also known as the detective approach or threat-based approach, is defined as the ability to resist specific identified threats to an asset. The threat-based (losing the asset) approach is where the risks and threats are identified to eliminate, and emphasise security monitoring of systems, networks and user behaviour for anomalies. It is, therefore, the ability to mitigate the identified threats for an asset.

Both approaches are essential for a well-balanced security strategy, in which the proactive approach aims to reduce the likelihood of incidents, and the reactive approach helps to identify and respond to incidents.

A well-balanced information security programme incorporates elements of both approaches to provide robust protection and a stable security strategy, in which the proactive approach aims to reduce the likelihood of incidents, and the reactive approach helps to identify and respond to incidents.

Security objectives – the CIA Triad

The positive or objective-based approach is to achieve the security goals below, known as the CIA Triad:

- **Confidentiality** – prevention of unauthorised information release.
- **Integrity** – prevention of unauthorised information modification.
- **Availability** – prevention of unauthorised denial of use.

Security violations

The negative or reactive approach to security violation, the threat-based approach has these three types:

- **Unauthorised information release** – protecting the confidentiality.
- **Unauthorised information modification** – protecting the integrity.
- **Unauthorised denial of use** – protecting the availability.

While the positive or preventive approach aims to reduce the likelihood of security incidents, the negative or detective approach helps to identify and respond to incidents that may occur despite preventative measures. A well-balanced information security programme incorporates elements of both approaches to provide robust protection and incident response capabilities.

Parkerian Hexad[1]

The Parkerian Hexad, introduced by Donn B. Parker in 1998, is a framework that extends the traditional CIA Triad (confidentiality, integrity and availability) to include three additional principles for a more comprehensive model (Figure 3.4). The six principles of the Parkerian Hexad are:

---

1   https://en.wikipedia.org/wiki/Parkerian_Hexad

Figure 3.4 The CIA Triad and Parkerian Hexad (Copyright: I-Perceptions Consulting Ltd)

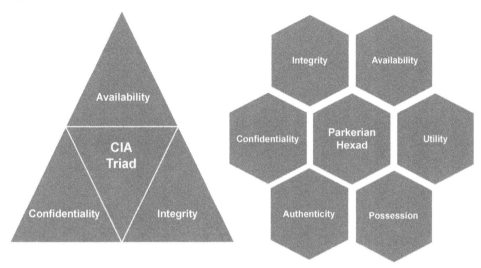

- **Confidentiality** – protecting information from unauthorised access.
- **Possession** – extends the confidentiality to include who owns and controls the data.
- **Integrity** – protecting information from unauthorised modification.
- **Authenticity** – extends the integrity in assuring that the source of information is authentic and can be verified.
- **Availability** – protecting information from unauthorised denial of use.
- **Utility** – extends the availability in ensuring that information remains functioning and serving the intended purpose and is not inaccessible.

ADDITIONAL SECURITY GOALS

In addition to the CIA Triad and Parkerian Hexad, other security goals contribute to a comprehensive and well-rounded approach to information security. These additional security goals complement and contribute to a holistic and effective information security strategy depending on the organisational context. Some of these, and not an exhaustive list, include:

- **Privacy** – to protect individuals' personal information (PI) or PII and ensure that it is handled appropriately and in compliance with privacy regulations. Data anonymisation, encryption and access controls contribute to privacy goals.
- **Compliance** – to ensure that organisations adhere to relevant law and regulatory requirements and industry standards governing the protection of information and data, such as compliance with data protection laws, financial regulations and industry-specific security standards.

- **Accountability** – to hold individuals or entities accountable for their actions by logging in with their credentials, maintaining an audit log for their actions and tracking their activities.

- **Reliability** – to build dependable systems, networks and robust infrastructure to reduce the risk of service interruptions and ensure continuous access to critical resources. Reliability is at the periphery regarding security goals and, in most cases, delivered within the broader context of availability. Reliability contributes to availability by emphasising the consistency and dependability of systems and services.

- **Incident management** – to implement agreed and documented processes and procedures for managing and mitigating security incidents. This could encompass pre-empting, preparing, responding, reporting, managing and learning from security incidents.

- **Business continuity plan (BCP)** – the goal of a BCP is to minimise downtime and recover quickly from disasters while keeping critical operations going. Disasters could include natural, cyber attacks, equipment failures or other unforeseen events. A BCP outlines the strategies and procedures to ensure that critical operations can continue during and after a disruptive incident.

Von Solms's 12 dimensions of information security

In addition to the security goals, Von Solms's 12 dimensions of information security will help to further widen the information security perspective.

In addition to his paper titled 'Information Security', published in 2001, Professor Rossouw Von Solms, a notable figure in the field of information security, made significant contributions to the understanding of information security.

He identifies 12 dimensions of information security that provide a comprehensive framework for understanding the various aspects and concerns related to information security. The 12 dimensions of information security, as outlined by Von Solms, are:

1. Security policy and strategy – this dimension involves the development of security policies and strategies that guide an organisation's approach to information security.

2. Information security management – encompasses the overall management of information security efforts within an organisation, including the establishment of an information security management system (ISMS).

3. Security organisation – is the structure and organisation of the security function, including roles and responsibilities for managing and enforcing security policies.

4. Asset classification and control – is identifying, classifying and controlling access to sensitive information assets within the organisation.

5. Personnel security – addresses the human factor in security, including background checks, training and awareness programmes for employees.

6. Physical and environmental security – is protecting information systems and data by securing physical facilities such as data centres and offices.

7. Access control – is managing and controlling access to information systems and data to prevent unauthorised access.

8. Systems development and maintenance – is ensuring that security considerations are integrated into the entire software development and system maintenance life cycle.

9. Business continuity management – is planning for the continuation of business operations in the event of a disruption or disaster, with a focus on information security.

10. Compliance – is ensuring that the organisation complies with relevant laws, regulations and standards related to information security.

11. Incident management – is establishing procedures for detecting, responding to and recovering from security incidents and breaches.

12. Security metrics and information security governance – is measuring the effectiveness of security controls, monitoring security performance and establishing a governance structure for information security (Von Solms, 2000).

According to Von Solms, the above dimensions provide a comprehensive framework for addressing various aspects of information security to develop a more holistic and effective approach to protecting information assets and managing security risks.

Abhishek Narain Singh and M.P. Gupta, in their research article, 'Information Security Management Practices: Case Studies from India', note that the evolution of the information security discipline, as discussed by Von Solms, has developed in waves (Singh and Gupta, 2017).

The first wave was the 'technical wave'. As the name suggests, it revolved around technology to manage information security – the 1980s mainframe era with built-in security features such as user-IDs, passwords and access control lists.

From then to the mid-1990s, with the internet and distributed computing, organisations' boundaries becoming blurred led to the second wave, which is the 'management wave' – getting the attention of the senior management, realising the importance of information security and thereby introducing security policy and training programmes.

The first and second waves gave rise to the third wave, the 'institutional wave', focusing on the best practices and standardisation of information security management such as BS 7799 (from British Standards) and ISO/IEC 17799 (from the joint technical committee of the International Organization for Standardization and International Electrotechnical Commission).

Following this was the 'governance wave', emphasising corporate governance responsibilities such as security objectives and strategies, organisational structure, risk management and regulatory and compliance enforcement for managing information security.

Von Solms also debates the next wave (2000), called the 'commodity wave', where information security is like any other commodity and no longer an issue. However, he challenges himself to whether this wave could be a reality when information security is no longer on the radar due to the human dimension.

Elucidating CIA

Before proceeding to the final sections of this chapter, let's explore a selection of examples (though not exhaustive) that illustrate how data confidentiality (unauthorised information release), integrity (unauthorised information modification) and availability (unauthorised denial of use) can be compromised. These examples provide a glimpse into the width and depth of information security violations, which will in turn help strengthen the security mindset.

Data breaches
An attacker gains unauthorised access to a company's database containing customers' personal and sensitive information, such as names, addresses, credit card details and so on, causing loss of customer trust, financial loss, legal consequences and damage to reputation.

Phishing attacks
An attacker tricks individuals into revealing sensitive information, such as usernames and passwords, by posing as a trustworthy entity, causing unauthorised access to accounts, potential data breaches and compromised personal and sensitive information.

Data interception and eavesdropping
An attacker intercepts communication, such as phone calls or network traffic, and data in transit, such as unencrypted communication over a network, to access confidential information, causing compromised personal and sensitive conversations and resulting in exposure to classified information, legal consequences and damage to reputation. The following chapters provide more details on data in transit and at rest.

USB dropping
An attacker leaves infected USB drives in public places, hoping that someone will plug them into a computer and thereby unknowingly spread malware, compromise data and create unauthorised access to systems, resulting in data breaches, compromised personal sensitive information and disruption.

Brute force attacks
An attacker attempts to gain unauthorised access to an account or system by systematically trying all possible passwords, causing compromised confidentiality and resulting in data breaches, financial loss, legal consequences and damage to reputation.

Data tampering
An attacker gains unauthorised access to a database and tampers with the financial records, such as transactions, amounts or balances, causing incorrect information in the database and leading to loss of customer trust, financial loss, legal consequences and damage to reputation.

Document tampering
An attacker alters important documents, such as contracts or legal agreements, and manipulates terms and conditions, which causes legal disputes, financial losses and damage to reputation.

Code or file tampering

An attacker injects malicious code into software, systems or applications, leading to unauthorised modifications in the system or application behaviour that create compromised system behaviour and result in data breaches.

Website tampering

An attacker gains access to a website and replaces the original content with their own, often defamatory content, creating damage to reputation and potential legal consequences.

Database injection or tampering

An attacker injects malicious SQL commands to manipulate or extract data from a database, causing unauthorised access to sensitive information, data breaches, legal consequences and damage to reputation.

Supply chain attacks

An attacker compromises the integrity of software or hardware during the manufacturing or distribution process, causing compromised systems behaviour and resulting in data breaches, legal consequences and damage to reputation.

Insider threats

An employee with authorised access intentionally or unintentionally tampers with data, causing a data breach and resulting in financial loss, loss of customer trust, legal consequences and damage to reputation.

Ransomware attacks

An attacker demands ransom for decryption keys by encrypting files using malware, causing loss of access to organisation data, prolonged systems downtime, performance degradation or complete system failure resulting in disruption of operations, financial loss, breach of sensitive information, legal consequences and damage to reputation.

Social engineering attacks

An attacker manipulates individuals into making unauthorised changes to systems, causing loss of access to organisation data and resulting in financial loss, breach of sensitive information, legal consequences and damage to reputation.

Distributed denial of service (DDoS) attacks

An attacker floods a system, network or website with traffic, overwhelming its capacity and causing a temporary or prolonged outage, causing disruption of services, loss of revenue and damage to reputation.

Physical theft and infrastructure attack

An attacker steals physical devices, such as computers, laptops and external drives, containing personal and sensitive information, or attacks the underlying infrastructure, such as data centres or cloud providers, impacting service availability and causing loss of classified information that results in data breaches, financial loss and damage to reputation.

Unfortunate attacks and natural disasters

An attacker triggers unfortunate events such as wars, natural disasters or accidents, or makes intended actions that cause power failures, thereby affecting the availability of systems and services and causing systems' downtime and disruption of services.

BUSINESS BENEFITS AND IMPACTS – TWO SIDES OF THE SAME COIN

While the dimensions and security goals mentioned above primarily concern cyber security analysts (Figure 2.2), having an understanding of them can also benefit business analysts when collaborating with security and IT teams.

Chapters 1 and 2 emphasised the significance of conducting comprehensive analyses. A key outcome of such thorough analysis is not only identifying the benefits generated by a proposed value but also recognising the impacts these benefits would yield – both positive and negative, intended and unintended.

While the focus is often on creating desired and intended benefits, it's crucial to acknowledge that impacts can sometimes be unintended. For instance, the integration of smart home devices promises enhanced convenience and automation for inhabitants (Laughlin, 2021). However, without adequate security measures, the unintended negative impact could involve malicious actors gaining unauthorised access to personal information, leading to data breaches. Another example is the Facebook 'Like' button feature, originally intended to share positivity. However, the social ramifications extend beyond this intention, with researchers uncovering broader psychological effects of social media interactions, particularly among teenagers (Eranti and Lonkila, 2015).

With the rapid pace of technology landscape expansion surpassing expectations, it's crucial that impact assessments not only focus on today's landscape but also strive to evaluate impacts across the breadth and depth of this expansion.

Seeing both the eye and everything around it

My gran told me this story when I was a child, and it has stayed with me. Although it didn't make much sense then, I remember it every time I perform an analysis.

This story is of Prince Arjuna, a renowned warrior celebrated for his exceptional bravery and mastery of archery in the Indian epic *Mahabharata*. As one of the five Pandava princes, Arjuna's prowess was legendary. One day their revered teacher, Dronacharya, instructed all the royal princes in the art of archery. Placing a wooden bird atop a tree branch, he tasked each student with aiming their arrows at the bird. Before releasing their arrows, Dronacharya queried each student about their focus. Responses varied: one saw the bird perched on the branch, another noticed the tree and yet another observed the tree along with the towering mountain behind it. However, when it was Arjuna's turn, he calmly asserted that he solely fixed his gaze upon the bird's eye, disregarding all else. True to his unwavering focus, Arjuna's arrow found its mark, striking the bird's eye with unmatched precision.

The story highlights the importance of maintaining unwavering focus on the goal – a lesson that resonates deeply with me. However, in my role as a business analyst, I must strike a delicate balance between meticulous attention to detail and a holistic view of the larger picture. Analysing individual changes while considering their ramifications on the entire system is a cornerstone of my work. My work requires me to navigate through intricate layers of complexity, zooming in to the minutiae while maintaining a bird's eye view, including the impacts (both positive and negative) at the forefront of my mind. I therefore need to look at the bird's eye, the bird and all the factors around that could potentially cause harm or be a threat in the scenario (Figure 3.5).

Figure 3.5 Circle of impact (Copyright: I-Perceptions Consulting Ltd)

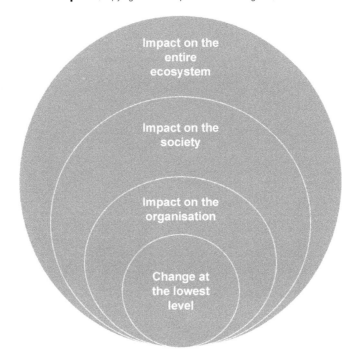

Recognising the importance of impact assessment, I have formulated a consistent approach that I employ each time to thoroughly evaluate both the benefits and impacts. This method entails scrutinising the effects of the business change not only on the product, but also on all interconnected systems within the technical and business landscape of the organisation. Moreover, it involves assessing the potential external impacts, extending beyond the organisational boundaries to encompass its ramifications on society and the broader ecosystem.

SUMMARY

Responding to the ever-changing social trends and business needs, frequent alterations and enhancements to technology and business processes is the need of the hour. Business analysts empowered with the security mindset, along with the security approaches, are well-positioned to meticulously weigh both the intended and unintended impacts of these changes. With these additional resources in their toolbox, they can effectively integrate cyber and information security considerations into their analyses, ensuring a comprehensive assessment and delivery of complete analyses. Subsequent chapters will delve deeper into the framework, techniques, and tools essential for this purpose.

TAKEAWAY QUESTIONS

- What are your key learning points in this chapter?
- What is the one lesson that you'll implement?
- How do you summarise your perspectives on security approaches?

4 WHERE IS THE TRAP?

Here's what you'll learn from this chapter:

- The first pillar – risk analysis.
- Risk is the central part of cyber security.
- Definition of risk.
- Approaches to risk management.
- Cyber resilience and risk management.
- Business analysis support to the risk management process.
- Other risk perspectives.
- Bias in risk.
- Barriers to effective risk management.
- AI in risk management.

THE TWO PILLARS

The previous chapter introduced the Business Analysis and Cyber Security Framework, emphasising the importance of establishing a foundational security mindset. In this chapter, we delve into the first of the framework's two key pillars: 'risk analysis' and 'business analysis' (Figure 4.1).

This chapter offers an in-depth examination of the risk analysis and management process, with a particular focus on business analysis touchpoints. The exploration aims to provide a holistic understanding, enabling you to identify biases and overcome barriers to facilitate effective risk management and decision-making.

The second pillar, business analysis, will be explored in the next chapter. It will highlight cyber security touchpoints across various phases of project delivery, ultimately contributing to the development of more secure and resilient systems and applications.

CONSCIOUS AND UNCONSCIOUS RISKS

Every day, whether we realise it or not, we make informal judgements on risks in our lives. From crossing a road to driving, using a phone or even sleeping, we encounter

Figure 4.1 Business Analysis and Cyber Security Framework with the two pillars
(Copyright: I-Perceptions Consulting Ltd)

situations where risk is a factor. Yes, even while sleeping, as there's no guarantee that everyone who sleeps will wake up the next day. Some risks we consciously take, while others we may not even be aware of or are unavoidable.

However, this informal approach to risk management doesn't suffice in an organisational context. When it comes to organisational risks, a formal risk management approach is essential to deal with organisational risks by making **risk the central part of cyber security**.

As in the previous chapters, this one, too, leans into a story to drive the key message. This story is from the book *Mastering Leadership the Mousetrap Way* by Manoj Vasudevan (2016).

The mousetrap

Once upon a time there lived a poor farmer. He lived in a small house with his wife. He had a small farm with a chicken, a goat and a cow. But there was another unwanted guest, a mouse. So, the farmer bought a mousetrap to get rid of his unwanted guest.

Seeing the mousetrap in the house, the mouse was alarmed and he ran out, panicking, to the farm to find help. He saw the chicken on the farm and asked for help as a mousetrap was in the house. The chicken, who was happily engrossed in pecking grains, stopped, looked at the mouse and said, 'I understand that this is a grave concern for you, but it is not my problem.'

Hearing this, the mouse was disappointed and continued to find help elsewhere. He saw the goat cheerfully running around the farm and asked for help. The goat stopped running at once, feeling sorry for the mouse, and said, 'Oh, it must be terrible for you, and I am sorry to hear your troubles, but it is not my problem.'

The mouse was terrified as he couldn't find help, but he didn't lose hope and persisted. He saw the merrily engrossed cow munching grass and asked her for help as a mousetrap was in the house. The cow opened her eyes, looked at the mouse, thought for a moment and said, 'Have you ever heard of a cow trapped in the mousetrap? I am sorry, but don't get me involved in your troubles. It is not my problem.'

The mouse, horrified and lost as he couldn't find help, went back to the house weeping, and retired for the day.

Before I continue this story, I encourage you to pause for a moment and identify all the risks inherent in this situation. These risks may pertain to any or all of the characters involved, and you're free to make assumptions as you see fit. I urge you not to overlook this crucial step – engaging in this reflective exercise will enable you to perceive risks from a different perspective. This reflective exercise will help you to see what is and is not visible, and you'll be glad you did it.

REFLECTION TIME

Take a moment, ponder and write down:

- What are the risks in this situation affecting any or all of the characters? Make assumptions as you see fit.

When everyone was asleep that night, there was absolute silence in the house. Then there was a loud noise from the mousetrap in the kitchen. Hearing this, the farmer's wife jumped out of bed and rushed to the kitchen. It was dark, and she couldn't contain her excitement. She stooped down to check the mouse trapped in the mousetrap, and to her astonishment it was a snake and not the mouse. The snake, in rage, bit her and she yelled in pain, waking up the farmer, who rushed to the kitchen and switched on the light. The farmer was dismayed to see his wife's dreadful situation and quickly did whatever he could to provide medical assistance. But the damage was already done.

His wife became terribly ill, and the doctor suggested he feed his wife chicken broth to help her recover, so the chicken had to go. Hearing about the wife's illness, their friends and family visited them, and now the farmer had to feed his guests, so the goat had to go as well.

His wife showed no sign of recovering and in a couple of days she passed away. The farmer not only had to bear the costs of her illness, but now, with the funeral costs, he had no other option other than to sell the cow, so the cow also had to go.

Losing his beloved wife, the farmer lost the will to live and he went into depression. In a few months, he too passed away. And the new boss of the house was the mouse (Vasudevan, 2016).

Did you foresee this ending to the story and were you able to identify any risks that materialised? Now take another moment to reflect on the story and the risks you identified earlier. Assess how accurately you gauged the threats to the characters. Has the story made you look more deeply and broadly into the situation?

Again, do not skip this process, as the exercise will deepen your learning to hone the skill of identifying both obvious and unobvious risks.

REFLECTION TIME

Take a moment, ponder and write down:

- How do you perceive risks after reading the story?
- Has it created a shift in seeing the obvious and the unobvious?

Among many key lessons from the story, the top three messages to drive home within the context of cyber security or security in general are:

- Security affects everyone, and therefore it is everyone's responsibility.
- A threat to an individual or a team in an organisation is a threat to the whole organisation, sooner or later.
- Leaders in organisations need to be prepared and not react in a panic. They need to anticipate the risks and be ready to respond accordingly.

However, it is a human tendency to overlook obvious risks, often assuming they won't materialise or, if they do, that they won't affect them personally. Hence, they are unprepared when these risks do materialise and that hits hard.

A quote widely attributed to Douglas Adams[2] brilliantly sums it up: 'The major difference between a thing that might go wrong and a thing that cannot possibly go wrong is that, when a thing that cannot possibly go wrong goes wrong, it usually turns out to be impossible to get at or repair.'

---

2   https://www.goodreads.com/work/quotes/42028477-the-hitchhiker-s-guide-to-the-galaxy-a-trilogy-in-five-parts

In this clever quote by Douglas Adams, he highlights the idea that things we assume won't break become irreparable once they do. In organisations too, when risks go unforeseen and subsequently manifest, the resulting damage is irreversible.

Although risk might appear simple, it gets complex in situations involving various moving parameters. The parameters get trickier as the situation changes, resulting in a confusing, endless loop.

But organisations today increasingly rely upon complex information systems and therefore a formal and structured approach becomes imperative, with risk emerging as a central concept in information security management.

Security is all about managing risks. We can call something secure only when all its risks are managed. And we can manage something only when it is identified. When a security breach or an incident is analysed, the root cause, in most cases, will directly or indirectly highlight mismanagement and overlooked risks, making 'identifying risks' critical because we don't know what we don't know, or, quoting Gary Cohn, vice Chairman of IBM:[3]

> 'If you don't invest in risk management, it doesn't matter what business you're in, it's a risky business.'

DEFINITION OF RISK

Risk identification requires curiosity and an open mind to ask many 'why' questions, one of the business analyst's essential activities, and that is when the things that can go wrong are identified.

The definition of risk by Businessdictionary.com is apt. Risk is 'a probability or threat of damage, injury, liability, loss or any other negative occurrence that is caused by external or internal vulnerabilities, and that may be avoided through preemptive action.' The definition not only defines risk but also highlights pre-emptive action. Pre-emptive thinking is a skill that requires training to see the visible and that which is not yet visible.

RISK MANAGEMENT PROCESS

It is now established that risks are the core of security management. The next part of this chapter briefly spotlights the process, along with risk bias and barriers, that the organisation should be mindful of when designing an effective risk management process.

The risk management process is not a one-time affair, but a cyclic process applicable to any risk in general.

---

3   https://www.moneyandbanking.com/commentary/2019/3/10/what-risk-professionals-want

The diagram in Figure 4.2 illustrates the ISO 31000 approach to enterprise risk management. ISO standards are a set of international standards developed by the International Organization for Standardization. ISO is an independent, non-governmental international organisation that develops and publishes standards to ensure the quality, safety and efficiency of products, services and systems across various industries.

Figure 4.2 Risk management process (Copyright: I-Perceptions Consulting Ltd)

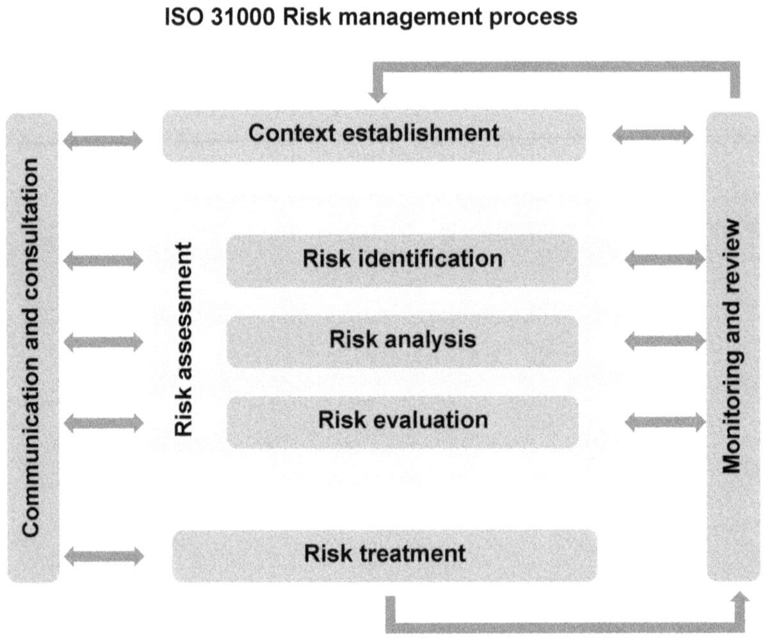

ISO 31000 Risk management process

An overview of the ISO 31000 risk management process is presented below, with guidance on the business analyst's role at every stage.

Establishing the context

In business analysis, it is imperative that a context or scope is set, and here, too, a context or scope is the first step in the risk management process. It encompasses identifying assets (physical or information) and assigning an owner to each asset as the initial step. The owner will be responsible for dealing with this risk when it materialises by making the necessary decisions and taking the necessary actions. They are also responsible for the maintenance and security of the asset.

Business analyst support
Business analysts can support this by analysing the organisation's business context, objectives and the external and internal environments and identifying the information security needs in collaboration with the security and IT stakeholders. The analysis also includes understanding the organisation's structure, processes, information assets and regulatory obligations. They can help to identify the risks when the context is clearly understood.

Risk assessment

As illustrated in Figure 4.2, risk assessment consists of three activities:

- risk identification;
- risk analysis;
- risk evaluation.

Risk identification

Risk identification aims to determine what could go wrong and to what extent the potential damage or loss could impact the organisation. It is about identifying and listing all the threats and vulnerabilities and their sources.

Business analyst support
Business analysts can facilitate workshops and discussions to identify and document risks, including information security risks, across all the systems and processes in the organisation. They also can conduct stakeholder analysis to identify and understand the perspectives, interests and potential risks associated with different stakeholders, which helps to anticipate and address stakeholder-related risks. Business analysts, in collaboration with the security and IT teams, can identify and document assets, vulnerabilities, threats and potential impacts in a risk register, using analytical techniques such as SWOT (strengths, weaknesses, opportunities, threats) and PESTLE (political, economic, sociological, technological, legal and environmental) analysis to uncover potential threats and opportunities.

Risk analysis

The identified risks undergo analysis based on the criticality of the assets involved. This analysis aims to determine both the frequency and probability of the threat manifesting and the potential extent or magnitude of the impact if the threat were to materialise. These risks are then categorised either qualitatively or quantitatively. Finally, the overall business impact is assessed, which involves factors including financial and operational, and non-tangible impacts such as reputational or impacting an individual's life, livelihood, society or ecosystem.

Business analyst support
Business analysts can play a crucial role in collaborating with stakeholders to assess and analyse identified risks, evaluating their likelihood, impact and overall business implications. They are adept at performing both qualitative and quantitative analyses to determine the level of risk exposure. They can support stakeholders in prioritising the risks based on their potential impact on project objectives. By offering valuable insights, they help stakeholders to make informed decisions to strategically manage the most critical and high-impact risks.

Risk evaluation

The third step of the assessment is risk evaluation, a process of making informed decisions regarding risk treatment and response strategies. It involves determining the significance of the analysed risks and prioritising them based on their potential impact on achieving the business or project objectives.

Business analyst support

Business analysts can support prioritising the risks based on their potential impact on business or project objectives and in the decision-making process to manage the most critical risks.

They can develop risk mitigation plans by suggesting alternative approaches, proposing changes to project scope, schedule or resources, identifying dependencies and assessing the feasibility of risk mitigation decisions and strategies.

Risk treatment

As illustrated above, the risk treatment process is the next phase in the ISO 31000 risk management process. It involves strategies and activities to manage the risks following their effective assessment. Risk treatment aims to reduce the likelihood or impact of the risks to levels acceptable to the organisation and aligned with its risk appetite. A risk treatment is identified, which could be to accept the risk, avoid it, reduce it or modify it, and share or transfer the risk depending on the nature and context within the organisation.

Risk acceptance is consciously and objectively accepting the risks, doing nothing about them now and responding if they manifest. It is acknowledging that a certain level of risk is acceptable. For example, making a decision not to invest in additional security measures for a low-impact system that does not store sensitive information.

Risk avoidance entirely prevents a particular risk by avoiding or withdrawing from activities, situations or circumstances that could cause that risk to manifest. For example, avoiding using a vulnerable system or piece of software no longer supported by the vendor or when the costs of implementing the treatment exceed the benefits.

Risk reduction is a strategy to reduce the likelihood or impact of a risk by bringing the risk level down to a more acceptable level, known as the residual risk. Risk reduction helps organisations strategically balance managing risks and achieving their objectives. For example, security controls and measures implemented, such as encryption, authentication firewalls, etc., reduce the likelihood and impact of a cyber security incident.

Risk sharing is sharing the responsibility of the risk with other parties, such as insurers or suppliers. The strategy is to distribute the risk among different entities to mitigate or lessen the financial load on the organisation. Risk sharing or transfer can be partially or fully outsourced. For example, outsourcing either a part of or complete payment processing capabilities or obtaining cyber security insurance to transfer the financial consequences of a data breach to an insurance provider mitigates the impact on the organisation's financial resources.

Business analyst support

Business analysts can conduct a cost–benefit analysis to assess the effectiveness and feasibility of risk reduction measures by evaluating the costs associated with implementing risk reduction strategies against the potential benefits in terms of risk reduction.

They can assist in prioritising the identified risk treatment options based on their alignment with organisational objectives and identify resource constraints and the potential trade-offs between different treatment strategies.

They can assess the effects of risk treatments on current business processes or the introduction of new processes, as well as anticipate the potential ripple effects on project scope, timelines, budgets and deliverables.

Business analysts can support project managers in creating detailed risk treatment plans that outline the actions, responsibilities, timelines and resources required to implement the selected risk treatment strategies. They then need to update the requirements catalogue and other relevant project documentation to ensure the changes are implemented within the processes and systems.

They can liaise between technical and non-technical stakeholders to achieve a shared understanding of risks and their management strategies, and facilitate communication and decision-making.

Monitoring and review

Risks are not static. The likelihood and impact constantly fluctuate, depending on the organisation's internal and external environment. Hence, regular monitoring is necessary to detect changes at an early stage and maintain the overall risk posture. Monitoring and reviewing ensures that the organisation remains adaptive and responsive to changes, with continuous improvement based on review feedback.

Business analyst support
Business analysts can support the establishment of mechanisms for continually monitoring the identified risks and the effectiveness of risk treatment plans. They can support in developing reporting mechanisms that provide insights to decision-makers and support ongoing improvement.

They can collaborate with stakeholders to define key performance metrics and indicators related to risk management processes, and facilitate the design of dashboards or reporting mechanisms.

They can also support monitoring of the status of identified risks throughout the project life cycle, assist in tracking the effectiveness of risk mitigation strategies and provide regular updates to stakeholders and project teams. Reporting on risk status helps in maintaining awareness and facilitating timely decision-making.

Communication and consultation

Finally, effective communication and consultation are critical components of a successful risk management framework, promoting transparency and a shared understanding of the organisation's overall risk posture. It helps to ensure that the organisation benefits from the collective knowledge and insights. It also contributes to building a risk-aware culture, fostering trust among stakeholders and creating an environment to see risk management as a shared responsibility.

Business analyst support

Business analysts can collaborate with stakeholders to develop a communication plan for risk management. They can assist in defining communication objectives, identifying key messages, determining appropriate communication channels, and establishing a timeline for communication activities.

They can assist in preparing clear and concise documentation related to the organisation's risk management framework, processes and outcomes.

Business analysts can design and implement effective feedback mechanisms to elicit risk-related information by creating surveys, conducting interviews and facilitating workshops to capture stakeholder insights and concerns.

Business analysts can play a key role in ensuring the successful implementation of a risk management initiative. They can contribute to creating a risk-aware culture within the organisation with their ability to bridge technical and business perspectives, facilitate discussions and promote effective communication among stakeholders and decision-makers.

They can analyse data related to risk assessments, incidents and risk treatment plans. Business analysts can identify trends, patterns and areas of concern, and generate comprehensive reports for decision-makers. They can help to select, implement and optimise tools that streamline the monitoring and reporting of risk-related data. Using business analysis techniques to identify root causes, business analysts can help to assess the effectiveness of risk treatments and recommend improvements.

Business analysis can also collaborate with internal and external audit teams to facilitate audits of risk management processes and assist in preparing documentation, responding to audit findings and implementing corrective actions. They can also help to design scenarios, support testing activities and analyse results to identify areas for improvement, among others.

In addition, *Information Risk Management* (Sutton, 2021) is a comprehensive guide that can help business analysts to gain deeper insights into comprehending and mitigating various risks associated with information.

MAINTAINING CYBER RESILIENCE

A well-established risk management process is foundational to achieving cyber resilience. Cyber resilience is the ability of an organisation to holistically prepare to respond and recover from cyber threats, cyber attacks, data breaches, system failures and other security incidents. A robust risk management process is instrumental to maintaining cyber resilience in an organisation. The risk management process provides the framework for identifying, assessing, mitigating and monitoring risks – critical components of a comprehensive cyber resilience strategy.

OTHER RISK PERSPECTIVES

With a good understanding of an effective risk management process, it is essential to understand some do's and don'ts.

Although it had become a common practice in some organisations to ignore the low-likelihood risks, especially those with high-impact, existential risks, the Covid pandemic and recent wars have reminded us that however low the likelihood or probability of the existential risks could be, **they are never zero**. These events are a wake-up call to recognise the social, economic and environmental changes taking place at the fastest pace ever recorded in the history of humankind.

While high-consequence, low-likelihood risks cannot be ignored, preparing for every probable risk is impossible, expensive and impractical. Therefore, organisations must develop strategies to help them prioritise and prepare for those high-impact risks relevant to their organisational context. However, the challenge is developing the strategy, especially when the future is unknown.

In their article, 'The disaster you could have stopped: preparing for extraordinary risk', McKinsey's Fritz Nauck, Ophelia Usher and Leigh Weiss, recommend conducting a 'premortem exercise', a technique risk decision-makers can employ to identify which 'predictable surprises' would have severe consequences for their organisation (Nauck et al., 2020). 'Predictable surprises' is the phrase Michael Watkins and Max Bazerman coined in their *Harvard Business Review* article (Watkins and Bazerman, 2003). They are those high-impact and low-probability risks affecting the organisation's value proposition to which the organisations need to respond when manifested.

Furthermore, in a podcast episode from McKinsey's *Inside the Strategy Room* (Aufreiter et al., 2022), Nora Aufreiter, Celia Huber and Ophelia Usher bring a board perspective to the board's role in ensuring readiness for existential risks by suggesting these activities:

- The first is identifying the 'predictable surprises' and defining pre-emptive actions.
- The second is to look at risks through the lens of scenarios. Creating well-planned and laid-out scenarios of the predictable surprises would provide insight into the impacts. A scenario can have multiple risks hitting it simultaneously, and those multiple stories help to open up the imagination and aid decision-making. The crux is in building imaginative scenarios backed up with data from market forecasts, expert opinions and world economic forum reports on how the organisation would be affected if those risks were to manifest in the short and long term. Thinking ahead on the mitigations and being prepared is the name of the game.
- The third step is to prepare a well-balanced business resilience plan focusing on all dimensions, including financial, operational, technical, resources, reputation and business models. Prioritise the scenarios, allocate budget and resources to those and create processes for managing incidents and business continuity based on the risk appetite.
- The fourth step is being mindful and tactical to harness potential opportunities by creating business models to take advantage of and invest in them when those scenarios manifest. A classic example is Amazon helping third parties build e-commerce sites, leading to Amazon Web Services (AWS). According to AAG IT, AWS has around 30 per cent of the cloud-computing market share (Griffiths, 2024).

Business analyst support

Business analysts, with their hard and soft skills, can offer support in identifying the predictable surprises. They can facilitate creating the scenarios to help illustrate the impacts of these predictable surprises on the organisation, employees, customers, suppliers, society or the ecosystem. Business analysts can influence the organisation by collaborating with the decision-makers at the strategic level and emphasising the organisation's overall resiliency. The investments that organisations make to protect their value propositions or potential opportunities can mean the difference between survival and extinction.

> The investments that organisations make to protect their value propositions or potential opportunities can mean the difference between survival and extinction.

BIAS IN RISK

Human beings are the product of their upbringing and environments, resulting in cognitive bias, which plays a significant role in perceiving, interpreting and responding to risk, leading to errors in judgement and decision-making. Therefore, awareness of risk bias is another crucial aspect to foster for a more objective and accurate assessment of risks.

The Institute of Risk Management (IRM) has developed a short guide[4] to combat bias in risk management, as listed below:

Availability bias is the dependence on information where individuals heavily depend on information that is easily accessible or comes to mind readily when assessing risks or making decisions. However, by assembling a group of challengers with diverse perspectives and backgrounds, this bias can be effectively mitigated.

Anchoring is relying too heavily on a single piece of information offered, which is referred to as an 'anchor' when assessing a risk or making a decision. Redoing the assessment with new reference data and examining the likely outcomes to be accurate helps to lessen anchoring bias.

Hindsight is the influence of previous experiences predicting the outcome, and the suggestion to avoid this is to capture as much data as possible and construct counterfactuals.

Groupthink is the inclination within a group to prioritise consensus over critical analysis, often motivated by a desire to avoid conflict. This can lead to flawed outcomes that are unanimously agreed upon, even if more preferable and plausible alternatives exist but are not unanimously accepted. Creating diverse and balanced groups can help counteract the biases inherent in groupthink.

---

4   https://www.theirm.org/media/2517624/1-short-guide-managing-bias.pdf

Overconfidence occurs when individuals or groups exhibit excessive confidence in their judgements, often leading them to overestimate the likelihood of certain events happening or not happening. Employing techniques such as downward counterfactuals (imagine scenarios in which outcomes are worse than what actually occurred) and premortems (a technique used to anticipate potential failures or problems before they occur) can help to mitigate this tendency.

BARRIERS TO EFFECTIVE RISK MANAGEMENT

The final aspect to consider for effective risk management is risk barriers. Identifying and addressing the barriers is crucial to fostering a proactive and resilient approach to uncertainties. Overcoming these challenges often involves a combination of cultural changes, improved communication and the allocation of adequate resources to support comprehensive risk management practices.

Below are some common barriers, although not an exhaustive list:

- Lack of awareness – not recognising the potential impact of risks or underestimating the need for a proactive risk management strategy.

- Communication gaps – lack of clear communication channels results in stakeholders not being aware of the identified risks and the corresponding mitigation strategies.

- Risk-averse culture – organisations resistant to change can impede effective risk management.

- Short-term focus – organisations focused on short-term gains may prioritise immediate objectives over long-term risk management strategies.

- Inadequate information – insufficient or outdated information can result in inaccurate risk identification and evaluation, compromising the effectiveness of risk management efforts.

- Overly complex risk management process – risk management processes that are too intricate may not be effectively integrated into everyday decision-making processes.

REFLECTION TIME

Take a moment, ponder and write down:

- Can you identify three risks that you would want to assess for risk bias?

- What are the risk barriers that you are dealing within your organisation?

- Has your perception towards risk changed? If yes, how has it shifted?

AI IN RISK MANAGEMENT

Before concluding this chapter, here is a peek into harnessing AI to further boost the risk management process. AI can significantly enhance risk management by providing advanced analytics, automation and predictive capabilities.

AI can perform data analysis with vast amounts of data from various sources to identify potential risks and patterns that may not be apparent through traditional methods, and can automatically detect anomalies and outliers that may indicate emerging risks.

With predictive analysis using historical data, AI can help to forecast future risks and their potential impact, assess the likelihood and severity of risks and enable you to prioritise and act on the most critical issues.

One way AI can be used is to analyse transactional data for fraud detection using machine learning (ML) models to analyse transactional data in real time, identifying patterns associated with fraudulent activities.

AI can analyse user behaviour and network activities to detect unusual patterns, and provide behavioural analytics that may indicate a cyber security threat. It helps in early identification and response to potential cyber risks.

Robotic process automation (RPA) can streamline routine risk management tasks, allowing human resources to focus on more complex analysis and decision-making, which improves efficiency and reduces the risk of manual errors in repetitive tasks.

AI can perform scenario analysis by creating simulation models to assess the potential impact of various events on the organisation to help them understand the consequences of different risk scenarios.

Real-time monitoring of data streams can alert organisations to potential risks and enable them to respond proactively. Combining AI's analytical capabilities with human insights can create a more robust and effective risk management process.

SUMMARY

This chapter covered various facets of risk management, distinguishing between conscious and unconscious risks and emphasising the importance of recognising both through the Mousetrap Way story.

The definition of risk with emphasis on pre-emptive action, followed by an exploration of the risk management process, a cornerstone for maintaining cyber resilience, is highlighted as a critical component that requires proactive measures and adaptive strategies in response to evolving cyber threats.

The concept of predictable surprises and the experts' recommendations underscored the significance of foresight in risk management, while discussions on bias in risk shed light on how cognitive biases can influence decision-making and highlighted some common barriers to effective risk management. The chapter concluded by touching on the role of AI in risk management, showcasing its potential to enhance and streamline processes for more efficient risk mitigation.

TAKEAWAY QUESTIONS

- What are your key learning points in this chapter?
- What is the one lesson that you'll implement?
- How do you summarise your perspectives on an effective risk management process?

5   THE STRUCTURED COMMON SENSE

Here's what you'll learn from this chapter:

- Common sense and business analysis.
- The second pillar – business analysis.
- IIBA knowledge areas with cyber security extension.
- IIBA BACCM with cyber security extension.

The Business Analysis and Cyber Security Framework unveiled in Chapter 3 emphasises cultivating the foundational security mindset. Chapter 4 unfolded one of the twin pillars, 'risk analysis', and in this chapter the spotlight shifts to the second pillar, 'business analysis'.

COMMON SENSE AND BUSINESS ANALYSIS

In the vein of former president of the United States James Madison's insight that philosophy is common sense with big words, I am inclined to believe that business analysis is common sense with structure. Every time I attend a business analysis training session, a profound realisation dawns that everything learned seems inherently logical, akin to common sense. Yet, I had to attend the training to realise and be reminded. Much as the imperative nature of cyber security or security at large is an integral aspect of everyone's responsibility, this, too, requires periodic acknowledgement and reinforcement to recalibrate our cognitive constructions. The elusive nature of common sense, a treasure not universally abundant, emerges as an invaluable asset across all professions, accentuating its pivotal role within the realm of business analysis.

> Philosophy is common sense with big words.
>
> Business analysis is common sense with structure.

The multifaceted landscape of business analysis demands an amalgamation of skills, techniques, tools and methodologies, all orchestrated to foster a disciplined and structured practice. Professional business analysts undergo training, acquiring specialised skills that empower them to effectively navigate the intricate terrain of analysing business needs. In essence, common sense, elevated to a structured plane, becomes the blueprint for effective business analysis.

THE SECOND PILLAR

Business analysts leverage many different models and frameworks including, but not limited to, the Ansoff Matrix, Debra Paul's Business Analysis Service Framework (BASF), Porter's Five Forces Model, IIBA's knowledge areas, Boston Consulting Group's Growth Share Matrix, PESTLE and SWOT analysis. Each of these models brings its unique focus areas, accompanied by distinctive strengths and weaknesses. Nevertheless, as the analysis unfolds, a common destination emerges, which is the shaping up of requirements essential for addressing the identified business needs. These diverse models and frameworks offer a structured and comprehensive approach to the intricate landscape of business analysis, guiding analysts through a systematic exploration of the business environment and the needs leading up to the solutions.

Storytime: The Three Little Pigs

This is one of the stories I read in my early school years, only to realise the meaning of the fable later in adulthood. The importance of checking the intention before an initiative, to check what is being built, will serve the intended purpose, is a critical factor especially within the business analysis context. The story has been slightly modified here to deliver the intended message.

Once upon a time, there were three little pigs. It was time for them to leave their home, make their way in the world and build houses for themselves. Their mother had guided and taught them well, and before they left she reminded them always to work hard and think before acting. The first little pig was lazy, chose the easier option to get by and paid too little heed to her advice. The second little pig tried to make sense of the advice but lost interest and gave up. The third little pig was wise and always was keen to take his mother's advice.

So, the three little pigs set off. They met a man carrying a bundle of straw, and the first little pig, without much thinking, bought the straw to build his house. The other two were not convinced and continued on their journey. Then they met a man carrying a bundle of sticks, and the second pig thought sticks were stronger than straw, so he bought the sticks to build his house. But the third little pig still wasn't convinced. He needed a stronger house to remain protected and continued on his journey. He met a man with a cartload of bricks. He thought this was what he needed to build a strong house and bought the bricks from the man.

All the three pigs now had their own houses.

A few days later, a hungry wolf came along and wanted to eat the pigs. He knocked on the straw house door and asked the first pig to let him in. When he wasn't let in, he blew the house down. The next day, the wolf returned, knocked on the stick house door and asked the second pig to let him in. When he wasn't let in, he blew again and the stick house went down. The following day, the wolf came back, knocked on the brick house door and asked the third pig to let him in. When he wasn't let in, he blew and nothing happened. He blew repeatedly, and still nothing happened to the house. So the wolf decided to enter the house through the chimney. As he was walking on the roof, the wise pig put a cauldron on the stove and started to boil the water. The wolf, who was trying to get in through the chimney, now had no chance as he would be scalded, and so he ran away for his life. The third pig, who had built a strong house, was safe.

The story brings out three important lessons, among others:

1. The need to clearly understand the intention behind the objective. Although the aim was to build a house, the intention was to be protected against dangers.

2. The need to clearly understand the dangers. Unless the nature of the threats is known, a suitable solution cannot be built.

3. It takes knowledge and effort to build the required solution.

The first pig wasn't prepared to put in the effort and went for the easy option, and the second pig didn't know how to make the right choice, so they were both unaware of the risks they were taking and eventually lost their houses and their lives. The third pig knew the threats and built a house that would protect him against those threats, and so was protected.

Business analysis frameworks provide a systematic and disciplined approach to address the business need, with knowledge, competencies, techniques and tools to identify, define and propose suitable solutions, like the strong brick house.

While there are various business analysis frameworks as mentioned above, this chapter addresses the IIBA knowledge areas, highlighting the cyber security extensions. IIBA's *Business Analysis Body of Knowledge* (2015) (BABOK v3) provides a comprehensive guide and framework for the practice of business analysis. It provides a set of knowledge areas, tasks, techniques and competencies essential for business analysis.

As per BABOK v3, knowledge areas are a collection of logically related tasks that describe a specific business analysis area. The diagram in Figure 5.1 displays the knowledge areas and the relationships between them.

IIBA'S BUSINESS ANALYSIS KNOWLEDGE AREAS

The next part of this chapter lists the knowledge areas, and notes the cyber security touchpoints. Remember, Chapter 2 established that business analysts can call upon cyber security SMEs as and when the project dictates. The key to recognising if any of the project aspects require cyber security SMEs is set out in Figure 2.3, 'Overview of cyber security knowledge for business analysts', so ensure those SMEs are involved to support the analysis accordingly.

Figure 5.1 IIBA knowledge areas (Copyright: International Institute of Business Analysis)

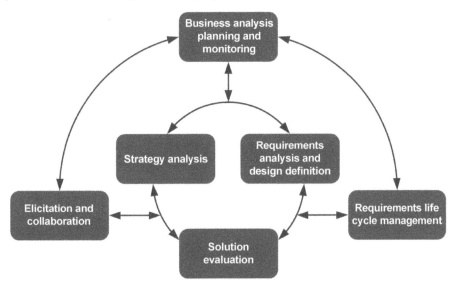

Business analysis planning and monitoring

The Business Analysis Planning and Monitoring knowledge area provides guidance on how to effectively plan and manage business analysis activities throughout a project or initiative to ensure that business analysis efforts are aligned with the overall project objectives and that the business analyst has a clear plan to execute their tasks.

As stated in BABOK v3, the Business Analysis Planning and Monitoring knowledge area includes planning the business analysis approach, planning stakeholder engagement, planning business analysis governance, planning business analysis information management and identifying business analysis performance improvements. The cyber security extension ensures that the business analysis plan incorporates cyber security measures, and that ongoing monitoring includes assessing the effectiveness of cyber security controls.

Extension to cyber security

Prerequisites Understanding the cyber security objectives within the organisation's overall business strategy, cyber security posture, concerns, risks, current measures, vulnerabilities and threat landscape. Recognising the potential impact of cyber security incidents on the business needs and the organisation.

Activities

- Supporting the identification and assessment of the cyber security risks associated with business analysis activities.

- Integrating the cyber security considerations into the scope and objectives of the business analysis plan.

- Planning for collaboration with cyber security stakeholders to ensure effective engagement and communication.
- Establishing governance processes to address relevant cyber security considerations within business analysis activities, such as decision-making processes for cyber security-related information.
- Managing cyber security-related information, specifically protocols for handling sensitive data.
- Integrating cyber security information management into the overall information management plan.
- Identifying cyber security-specific metrics and key performance indicators (KPIs) to align with the project and organisational security objectives.
- Integrating cyber security metrics into the overall monitoring and reporting mechanism to ensure that business analysis activities contribute to cyber security objectives.
- Integrating cyber security requirements traceability into the overall traceability plan.
- Defining an approach for creating, organising and maintaining business analysis documentation, which includes cyber security-related information.
- Helping to establish protocols for securing and handling sensitive cyber security documentation.
- Integrating cyber security documentation into the overall documentation plan.
- Defining review criteria and checklists that include cyber security considerations.
- Establishing review processes to ensure relevant compliance with cyber security standards.

Elicitation and collaboration

The Elicitation and Collaboration knowledge area provides guidance and best practices to ensure business analysts gather relevant and accurate information from stakeholders and foster collaboration throughout the business analysis process.

A successful elicitation and collaboration involves:

- Stakeholder engagement, which is identifying, communicating and managing stakeholders throughout the business analysis process.
- Collaboration, which is working together with stakeholders to achieve the business goals.
- Elicitation, which is the process of drawing out information from stakeholders to understand their needs, expectations and concerns.

As stated in BABOK v3, the Elicitation and Collaboration knowledge area includes preparing and planning for elicitation, conducting elicitation, confirming elicitation results, communicating the information and managing stakeholder collaboration. The cyber security extension ensures that the elicitation process accounts for security needs and adapts the elicitation and collaboration processes to include cyber security stakeholders.

Extension to cyber security

Prerequisites   Understanding the cyber security objectives within the organisation's overall business strategy, cyber security posture, concerns, risks, current measures, vulnerabilities and threat landscape. Recognising the potential impact of cyber security incidents on the business needs and the organisation.

Activities

- Conducting a stakeholder analysis to identify cyber security-focused roles and responsibilities. Identifying and engaging with stakeholders from security teams who play crucial roles in cyber security, such as IT security professionals, data privacy officers and compliance officers.

- Collaborating with the identified cyber security stakeholders to understand their specific needs and concerns.

- Planning for eliciting information related to cyber security policies, regulatory requirements and specific security controls aligning with the overall business analysis plan.

- Eliciting information related to cyber security risks, threats and vulnerabilities, and identifying requirements in collaboration with business and cyber security stakeholders.

- Confirming that elicited information addresses identified cyber security risks and concerns.

- Validating security requirements with cyber security stakeholders to confirm alignment with overall business requirements.

- Creating models to represent the flow of sensitive information, encryption mechanisms and access controls.

- Collaborating with stakeholders to prioritise cyber security decisions and implementations.

- Documenting cyber security requirements that address identified risks and align with overall business requirements.

- Documenting risk assessments, including identified threats, vulnerabilities and risk mitigation strategies.

- Reflecting on past cyber security incidents to identify areas for improvement in elicitation and collaboration techniques.

- Maintaining the confidentiality of information shared by stakeholders.

Requirements life cycle management

The Requirements Life Cycle Management knowledge area focuses on the processes and activities involved in managing requirements throughout the life cycle. It includes eliciting, documenting, analysing, prioritising and validating requirements, including tracking changes and ensuring the requirements align with the overall project and organisational goals.

As stated in BABOK v3, the Requirements Life Cycle Management knowledge area includes tracing requirements, maintaining requirements, prioritising requirements, assessing requirements changes and approving requirements tasks. The cyber security extension ensures that cyber security requirements are identified, documented, validated and managed methodically and effectively to maintain the security posture for safeguarding sensitive information, maintaining the integrity of systems and ensuring business continuity.

Extension to cyber security

Prerequisites   Understanding the cyber security objectives within the organisation's overall business strategy, cyber security posture, concerns, risks, current measures, vulnerabilities and threat landscape. Recognising the potential impact of cyber security incidents on the business needs and the organisation.

Activities

- Identifying cyber security requirements and explicitly documenting those as part of the overall requirements identification process.

- Collaborating with cyber security experts to identify relevant security requirements within the business processes.

- Documenting specific cyber security control requirements, such as encryption, access controls and authentication requirements, as part of the overall functional requirements.

- Documenting specific regulatory and compliance requirements related to cyber security impacting the business processes or data as part of the overall functional requirements.

- Developing a traceability matrix that links cyber security requirements to design elements, test cases and other project artefacts.

- Managing changes and assessing the impact on cyber security controls.

- Collaborating with cyber security stakeholders when prioritising requirements to ensure critical and high-impact security requirements are assigned the appropriate priority levels by the cyber security stakeholders.

- Facilitating requirements reviews with cyber security stakeholders to gain consensus on functional and non-functional requirements impacting cyber security requirements.

- Establishing a change control process, including impact assessment on cyber security requirements.

Strategy analysis

The Strategy Analysis knowledge area provides guidance to ensure that business analysis efforts support the overall strategic direction of the organisation.

As listed in BABOK v3, the Strategy Analysis knowledge area includes analysing the current state, defining the future state, assessing the risk and defining change strategy tasks. Aligning cyber security with organisational goals is essential for protecting data assets and sensitive information.

Extension to cyber security

Prerequisites   Understanding the cyber security objectives within the organisation's overall business strategy, cyber security posture, concerns, risks, current measures, vulnerabilities and threat landscape. Recognising the potential impact of cyber security incidents on the business needs and the organisation.

Activities

- Assessing the current state with cyber security considerations such as security posture, capabilities and vulnerabilities.

- Facilitating risk assessments on current business processes and systems with security considerations.

- Evaluating the effectiveness of existing cyber security controls implemented within the current business processes and systems.

- Defining cyber security goals and objectives within the overall business goals and objectives for the future state.

- Identifying and assessing cyber security risks associated with the proposed business changes and the transition to the future state.

- Defining change strategy with cyber security considerations such as resilience and organisation culture.

Requirements analysis and design definition

The Requirements Analysis and Design Definition knowledge area focuses on the processes and activities involved in analysing requirements and designing a solution by translating the business needs into a well-defined solution that can be implemented.

As stated in BABOK v3, the Requirements Analysis and Design Definition knowledge area includes specifying and modelling requirements, verifying requirements, validating requirements, defining requirements architecture, defining solution options, analysing potential value and recommending solutions. The cyber security extension ensures that the solution meets business needs and incorporates measures to protect against cyber threats.

Extension to cyber security

Prerequisites   Understanding the cyber security objectives within the organisation's overall business strategy, cyber security posture, concerns, risks, current measures, vulnerabilities and threat landscape. Recognising the potential impact of cyber security incidents on the business needs and the organisation.

Activities

- Creating visual models that include cyber security controls within the business process.

- Creating detailed cyber security requirements within overall functional requirements.

- Creating misuse cases along with use cases.

- Creating 'bad' actors as part of user personas.

- Creating vulnerable scenarios along with happy and alternate scenarios.

- Ensuring that cyber security assumptions and constraints are part of overall project assumptions and constraints and communicated to stakeholders, including cyber security.

- Verifying that the cyber security requirements are adhering to the relevant regulations and standards.

- Validating cyber security requirements by the relevant cyber security stakeholders to ensure that the requirements will lead to a resilient solution.

- Documenting the rationale behind cyber security design decisions along with all evaluated options.

- Identifying and documenting any temporary cyber security requirements for transitional processes and secure transition of the solution.

- Defining roles and responsibilities for managing a cyber security incident.

- Documenting incident detection and response mechanisms that align with the organisational security policies.

- Documenting processes for analysing and responding to emerging cyber threats.

- Incorporating cyber security into the ongoing analysis and design processes, and fostering continual collaboration between functional teams and cyber security experts throughout the development life cycle.

Solution evaluation

The Solution Evaluation knowledge area focuses on the processes and activities involved in assessing and validating the performance and value delivered by a solution to ensure that the implemented solution meets the business needs and provides the expected value and identified benefits to stakeholders.

As stated in BABOK v3, the Solution Evaluation knowledge area includes measuring solution performance, analysing performance measures, assessing solution limitations, assessing enterprise limitations and recommending actions to increase solution value. The cyber security extension ensures that the evaluation process accounts for cyber security measures, identifies potential security risks and verifies that the solution effectively mitigates those risks.

Extension to cyber security

Prerequisites   Understanding the cyber security objectives within the organisation's overall business strategy, cyber security posture, concerns, risks, current measures, vulnerabilities and threat landscape. Recognising the potential impact of cyber security incidents on the business needs and the organisation.

Activities

- Supporting the security and technical teams in defining cyber security performance indicators and metrics based on security objectives.
- Analysing data on security incidents, vulnerabilities and threat detection.
- Supporting data analysis teams to identify cyber security incidents or weaknesses.
- Collaborating with cyber security stakeholders to interpret security performance metrics.
- Using statistical analysis to draw insights from cyber security performance data to identify trends, patterns and areas of improvement.
- Collaborating with cyber security stakeholders to:
  - assess system weaknesses and impacts of the identified vulnerabilities on the solution's overall security;
  - consider changes in the threat landscape and emerging cyber threats;
  - assess how enterprise-level cyber security measures may impact the solution's ongoing security;
  - develop recommendations based on the analysis of cyber security limitations and vulnerabilities;
  - prioritise and implement recommended actions;
  - document the expected impact of the proposed changes on the solution;
  - collect feedback regarding the perceived effectiveness of security measures to compare the achieved cyber security benefits with the expected benefits outlined in the security objectives;
  - analyse the return on investment (ROI) for cyber security controls and countermeasures.
- Monitoring user compliance with established security policies and procedures, and identifying barriers to cyber security best practice adoption.
- Establishing a process for regular monitoring of cyber security performance indicators.
- Analysing historical data to identify trends or patterns in security incidents to enable informed decisions on enhancing the cyber security posture.
- Collaborating with cyber security stakeholders to evaluate the ability of cyber security controls to handle increased cyber threats to assess scalability.

Like the IIBA's knowledge areas, there are several other frameworks, such as the Business Analysis Service Framework, PMI-PBA (Project Management Institute – Professional in Business Analysis), that business analysts can use, or a prescribed set of business analysis tasks from SFIA6, Vongsavanh and Campbell, etc. The choice of framework depends on the organisational context, business needs and nature of the projects being undertaken. Business analysts may therefore use a combination of frameworks and methodologies to adapt to different projects and situations.

I have found that most frameworks and business analysis tasks lean towards a set of common elements, such as a need or problem to solve, a solution that solves the problem, stakeholders who are impacted and so on. IIBA's Business Analysis Core Concept Model (BACCM) summarises the common elements and is a versatile tool to use on its own or with other frameworks and knowledge areas. The diagram in Figure 5.2 exhibits the BACCM and the relationships between the elements.

Figure 5.2 IIBA BACCM (Copyright: International Institute of Business Analysis. All rights reserved)

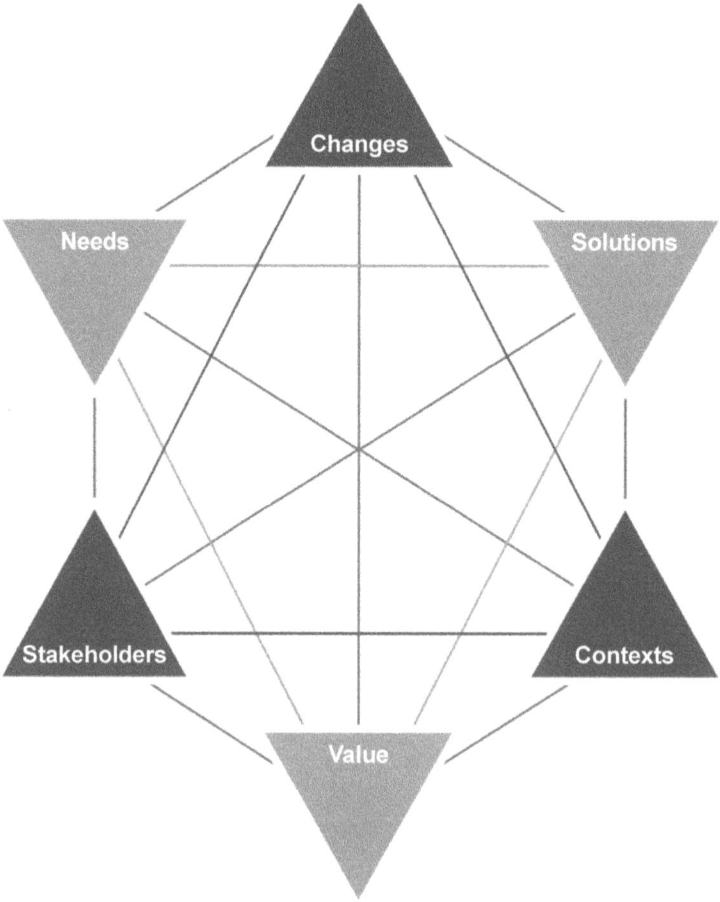

IIBA'S BUSINESS ANALYSIS CORE CONCEPT MODEL

The IIBA BACCM checklist is a 'value-added applied knowledge' resource available on the IIBA Knowledge Hub, and Table 5.1 is the cyber security extension in line with the IIBA BACCM checklist, which can be used either on its own or with other frameworks or business analysis tasks to assess cyber security impacts as part of the analysis.

Table 5.1 IIBA BACCM checklist cyber security extension

IIBA's Business Analysis Core Concept	Cyber security-related questions to consider
Stakeholders refers to an individual or group or organisation that have an interest in the decisions, operations or performance of a company or project and will have a relationship to the change, the need or the solution.	Are the cyber security stakeholders involved? Do the cyber security stakeholders have specific cyber security needs or requirements? Do the stakeholders need to be authorised or authenticated? Do the cyber security stakeholders have concerns about the change?
Context refers to the circumstances, conditions or settings that surround and give meaning to an event, an idea, a statement or a concept that influence or are influenced by and provide a rationale for the change.	Does the context involve the organisation's crown jewels? Will the limitations compromise or impact cyber security? What is the risk if it is not protected? Does the organisation's culture, behaviours and attitude towards cyber security compromise the security posture?
Need refers to the gap between the current state of the organisation and its desired state representing a problem or opportunity that the business aims to address.	Does the need include or impact cyber security? Does the problem include or impact cyber security? Does the opportunity impact cyber security? If the needs are conflicting, do they impact cyber security? Does the prioritisation compromise or impact cyber security? What is the risk if not actioned?

(Continued)

Table 5.1 (Continued)

IIBA's Business Analysis Core Concept	Cyber security-related questions to consider
Solution refers to a means or method of solving a problem or addressing a need identified within an organisation.	Does the solution raise any cyber security risks?
	If yes, how does the solution need to be protected?
	What level of protection is ideally suited for the solution?
Change refers to the process, act or instance of making modifications to business processes, policies, information systems, organisational structures or any other aspects of the business environment to address specific needs, solve problems or exploit opportunities.	Does the change raise any cyber security risks?
	Does the change impact any existing cyber security posture?
	Will the improvement need additional cyber security or governance requirements to be considered?
	Will the change strategy impact security objectives?
	What is the risk if not actioned?
	If the answer is yes to any of the above questions, then cyber security stakeholders must be consulted accordingly.
Value refers to the benefits or improvements realised by an organisation through the implementation of changes or solutions.	Does the potential value need to be protected, considering value can be tangible or intangible?
	How is the value perceived by the cyber security stakeholders?
	Are there any cyber security risk factors that impact the value?
	Are there any security-related metrics to assess the value of the solution?

SUMMARY

This chapter provided an exploration of the business analysis component that represents the second pillar within the Business Analysis and Cyber Security Framework. Through the integration of cyber security extensions into IIBA's knowledge areas and BACCM, the chapter listed cyber security activities to align with business analysis activities. It underscored the imperative collaboration with cyber security stakeholders, emphasising the need to adeptly identify and seamlessly integrate cyber security considerations into the overall business analysis process.

As we navigate forward, subsequent chapters will progressively delve into the remaining components of the Business Analysis and Cyber Security Framework.

TAKEAWAY QUESTIONS

- What are your key learning points in this chapter?
- What is the one lesson that you'll implement?
- How do you summarise your perspectives on effective business analysis activities with cyber security extension?

6   WHEN YOU PICK UP ONE END OF THE STICK, YOU ALSO PICK UP THE OTHER

Here's what you'll learn from this chapter:

- Shifting left.
- Value and protection – the two ends of the stick.
- Knowing where to tap.
- Right tools for the right job.

'Shift left' within the context of cyber security embodies the proactive approach of embedding security measures and protocols earlier in the software development and IT operations life cycle. This strategic move aims to tackle security vulnerabilities and risks at their nascent stages, well before deployment. By doing so, it effectively minimises the probability of security breaches and minimises their potential impact.

In order to address security vulnerabilities and risks at the earlier stages it is imperative that cyber security is part of those discussions and is baked alongside all other deliverables thoughout the project life cycle.

This chapter aims to address this by providing pointers to bring relevant cyber security conversations to the table at every stage of the project. Every organisational context is different and every project is different, hence there is no one-solution-fits-all approach to cyber security or security in general. Therefore the pointers provided in this chapter should be taken as guidelines to help trigger the security mindset and involve security expertise – asking the right questions and at the right time, shifting cyber security to the left and not as an afterthought.

VALUE AND PROTECTION – THE TWO ENDS OF THE STICK

By now, it is clearly established that anything of value needs to be protected. When you pick up one end of the stick, you also pick up the other end. This is a metaphorical way of conveying that actions or decisions often come with both positive and negative consequences or responsibilities. It suggests that, when you undertake a certain task or make a choice, you are also accepting the associated responsibilities and challenges that come with it. In essence, it underscores the idea that many situations involve a dual nature, and one must be aware of the entire scope of an action or decision, not just the immediate benefits or advantages. It encourages a holistic and mindful approach to decision-making, considering both sides of the metaphorical 'stick' before committing to a course of action.

When you undertake a certain task or make a choice, you are also accepting the associated responsibilities and challenges that come with it.

While technological advancements bring efficiency and convenience, they concurrently expose businesses to the risks of cyber threats. Organisations must recognise that safeguarding their enterprise against cyber threats is an integral part of the business endeavour in the digital age.

Storytime: Where to tap

One day a large factory came to a standstill when one of its boilers failed to work. Despite the efforts of the best engineers and mechanics, they couldn't figure out a solution to fix it. Exhausting all the options, the management called an old, retired boilermaker who was known for his exceptional skills and experience.

The old boilermaker arrived, intently listened to the problem, asked a few questions, looked at the troubled boiler, listened to it and then pulled out a small hammer from his toolbox. He tapped a specific spot on the boiler gently and, as he did that, to everyone's amazement the boiler started working perfectly again.

The old man then handed over an invoice of £1000 to the management. The management was outraged and perplexed at the invoice amount, as it had taken less than 15 minutes to fix it and all the boilerman did was tap with a hammer, and they requested an itemised bill. The boilermaker provided the details, which read:

- Tapping with a hammer: £10.
- Knowing where to tap: £990.

Many years back I heard this story (and the different versions); it was used to emphasise the experience and the know-how of business analysts, which is more important than the skill itself. It's a classic tale used to illustrate the importance of experience, expertise and intuition in problem-solving.

The old boilermaker didn't spend hours, as he relied on his years of experience to pinpoint the exact spot that needed attention. In business analysis, too, a skilled analyst with experience can swiftly identify issues or inefficiencies within business processes, systems or strategies.

They leverage their intuition and expertise to understand the complexities of a business, foresee potential challenges, identify strategic opportunities and propose effective solutions more efficiently, drawing from their knowledge of industry best practices and understanding of the specific business context.

It is practical wisdom, the ability to apply knowledge and experience judiciously, adapting analytical techniques to the specific needs and challenges of a given situation.

RIGHT TOOLS FOR THE RIGHT JOB

Business analysis has a myriad of tools and techniques, and using the right tool to address the right problem or the given situation is equally crucial for the success of the initiative.

The IIBA's BABOK v3 lists more than 50 techniques, and the third edition of the book *Business Analysis Techniques*, by James Cadle, Debra Paul, Jonathan Hunsley, Adrian Reed, David Beckham and Paul Turner (Cadle et al., 2021), lists 123 techniques.

Nevertheless, each technique brings its unique focus, strengths and weaknesses, and the effectiveness of these tools is intricately tied to the organisational context, the specific project phase and the business analyst's individual experience and comfort level.

The art of business analysis lies not only in understanding the diverse toolbox but also in the judicious selection of the most fitting tool or even parts of different techniques to make a new technique that may suit a specific situation for addressing the specific nuances of a given problem. Therefore, the adept business analyst is empowered to tailor their approach, recognising that the optimal choice of technique is a dynamic decision influenced by the intricacies of each unique circumstance.

While different project development methodologies can have variations in their phases, for the purpose of highlighting the techniques, the phases are broadly categorised into strategy analysis, design, development and testing phases. The following sections of this chapter provide an overview of the phases, outlining typical business analysis activities and a technique that is commonly used with cyber security extension.

Strategy analysis phase

The strategy analysis phase of a project lays the foundation in defining the overall direction of the project by understanding the context, setting objectives, defining the scope and establishing a strategic plan for successful project delivery.

Business analysts understand the context of the organisation and the problem being addressed by learning about the current state of the organisation, its processes and the challenges. They identify and analyse stakeholders who have an impact on or interest in the project by assessing their needs, expectations and concerns.

Cyber security extension

Integrating cyber security considerations into the strategy analysis ensures that the project is aware and prepared with strategies to protect its data assets and systems. Realising the need for protection of those valuable assets helps in prioritising cyber security efforts.

While business analysts may not be cyber security experts, they can play a crucial role in facilitating communication and collaboration between different stakeholders, including the cyber security, governance and business teams. They can support in:

- Identifying critical data assets and systems that need protection.

- Including cyber security stakeholders, during identifying and analysing overall project stakeholders.

- Performing a cyber security risk assessment with the cyber security team to identify potential cyber security risks and help to understand the cyber security landscape. While cyber security experts may lead the technical aspects of the cyber security risk assessments, business analysts can contribute by bridging the gap between technical and business perspectives.

- Helping to identify the strategies for relevant cyber security regulations and compliance, as applicable.

- Collaborating with business and security stakeholders in embedding security considerations into the project's objectives and goals to ensure that cyber security is an integral part of the project's strategic planning.

- Ensuring the cyber security requirements identified based on the risks and categorisations, such as confidentiality, integrity and availability, are integrated into project specifications.

- Developing appropriate risk treatments to protect against identified risks, such as access controls, encryption, auditing, network security measures, etc.

Tools and techniques
A few common techniques used during strategy analysis are Porter's Five Forces, PESTLE, STEEPLE, CATWOE, SWOT, VMOST and others. A couple of these techniques are elaborated below along with cyber security extension.

PESTLE
PESTLE analysis is built upon PEST analysis, a strategic tool for understanding market growth or decline, business position, potential and direction for operations. PEST was developed by J. Aguilar in 1967 as an environmental framework to scan the political, economic, social and technological categories that may affect strategy. The variant with 'legal' and 'environmental' factors, PESTLE, is one of the most common business analysis frameworks. It provides a structured approach for evaluating external factors impacting an organisation's performance and decision-making. By systematically analysing these factors, organisations gain a holistic view of the external environment, can shape their operating environment and adapt strategically to changes in the business environment.

- **Political factors** may include regulatory frameworks, tax policies, trade tariffs, political ideologies and political stability. Organisations need to assess the impact of political factors to consider the changes that may affect operations and the business environment.

  - **Cyber security extension** – assessing the political landscape regarding cyber security regulations and legislation that may impact the organisation, such as changes related to data protection and privacy, can have a significant influence on strategic decisions.

- **Economic factors** include inflation rates, exchange rates, interest rates, economic growth or recession, and overall economic stability. Organisations need to assess the economic factors to understand their potential impact on consumer behaviour, demand for products or services and financial stability.

- **Cyber security extension** – considering economic factors related to cyber security budgeting and resource allocation. Recessions or uncertainties may affect the organisation's ability to invest in expensive cyber security measures.
- **Social factors** include demographics, cultural attitudes, lifestyle trends, consumer behaviour and social values. Understanding social factors helps organisations to tailor their products, services and marketing strategies to the preferences and expectations of their target audience.
  - **Cyber security extension** – evaluating the level of cyber security awareness and culture within the organisation and the broader society. Understanding how different demographic groups may have varying levels of cyber security awareness and behaviours helps with aligning cyber security communication styles accordingly.
- **Technological factors** include innovation, automation, research and development, digital trends and the adoption of new technologies. Organisations need to stay abreast of technological changes to identify opportunities for improvement and assess potential disruptions in their industries.
  - **Cyber security extension** – expanding technology is the major risk for cyber security. Organisations must consider emerging cyber security technologies to enhance cyber security strategies and risk mitigations.
- **Legal factors** include employment laws, industry-specific regulations, intellectual property laws and compliance requirements. Organisations must ensure that their practices align with legal standards to avoid legal challenges and ensure ethical operations.
  - **Cyber security extension** – adherence to cyber and data related legal standards is crucial for strategic planning. Organisations must examine legal factors related to data protection and privacy laws, compliance requirements and potential legal consequences of cyber security incidents.
- **Environmental factors** include sustainability, climate change and environmental regulations. Organisations need to assess their environmental footprint and integrate environmental considerations into their strategic planning.
  - **Cyber security extension** – assessing cyber security in environmental factors involves understanding how sustainability, climate change and environmental regulations can impact an organisation's security posture; evaluate the environmental footprint of security measures such as data centres and network devices; and develop resilience plans by considering potential climate-related incidents such as extreme weather events.

VMOST

Another analysis planning tool is VMOST. It provides a structured framework for organisations to align their vision, mission, objectives, strategies and tactics to achieve their goals (VMOST). It was developed by Rakesh Sondhi, a business consultant, in his book, *Total Strategy* (Sondhi, 2008). The detailed description of VMOST with examples can be found in the book *Business Analysis Techniques* (Cadle et al., 2021).

- **Vision** is the overarching, aspirational statement that describes the organisation's desired future state, outlines what the organisation aims to achieve and provides a sense of direction.
  - **Cyber security extension** – introducing a cyber security vision that aligns with the overall organisational vision, outlining the desired future state of cyber security and the security posture within the organisation.
- **Mission** is a concise statement that articulates the organisation's purpose, values and the core reasons for its existence, outlining what the organisation does to achieve the vision.
  - **Cyber security extension** – developing a concise statement that articulates the organisation's commitment to cyber security, emphasising the protection of sensitive information and critical systems and maintaining the security posture.
- **Objectives** are concrete, measurable goals derived from the mission and vision that the organisation aims to achieve within a specific timeframe, and serve as the benchmarks for evaluating the organisation's performance and progress.
  - **Cyber security extension** – identifying cyber security objectives that are derived from the mission and vision to ensure that cyber security goals contribute to the organisation's overall objectives.
- **Strategies** are the high-level plans and approaches the organisation employs to achieve its objectives. They provide a roadmap for achieving the defined objectives by choosing the best courses of action.
  - **Cyber security extension** – ensuring that the chosen cyber security strategies align with the organisation's overall strategic plans and contributing to the achievement of strategic objectives.
- **Tactics** are the detailed, short-term practical steps, specific actions and activities to be undertaken to implement the chosen strategies. There can be multiple tactics to achieve an objective, or a tactic can contribute to one or more strategies, with metrics identified and monitored regularly to evaluate their effectiveness.
  - **Cyber security extension** – defining specific cyber security tactics and actions that support the chosen strategies, such as deploying security software and maintaining it with updated patches, conducting regular security audits, etc.

Integrating cyber security within VMOST analysis ensures that the organisation is not only focused on achieving its vision and mission but also committed to safeguarding the security posture and the overall resilience against cyber threats. In addition, it highlights the embraced security culture with the organisation and emphasises that cyber security is considered as an integral part of the organisational landscape.

Design phase

Following the strategy analysis phase, the design phase activities encompass elaborating on the requirements and designing solutions. Business analysts collaborate with stakeholders to ensure that the designed solution aligns with the organisation's needs by translating business and stakeholders' requirements into detailed specifications through visual representations, as necessary, such as to-be process flows, data models, use cases, functional and non-functional requirements, user stories and acceptance criteria, among others. The nature of the representation may be a document (or set of documents), but can vary widely depending on the circumstances and requirement categories.

In their book *Business Analysis* Debra Paul and James Cadle (2020) categorise requirements into the four types:

- **General requirements** are the business constraints, business policies, business continuity, legal, branding, cultural and language-related requirements.

- **Technical requirements** are the hardware, software, interface and internet-related requirements.

- **Functional requirements** are the data entry, maintenance, procedural and retrieval requirements.

- **Non-functional requirements** are the performance, security and access, backup and recovery, archiving and retention, robustness, availability, usability, accessibility and capacity and scalability requirements.

BABOK v3 states that 'a requirement is a usable representation of a need.' Requirements focus on understanding what kind of value could be delivered if a requirement is fulfilled and categorises requirements into business, stakeholder, solution and transition requirements.

- **Business requirements** are the high-level needs, goals and outcomes describing the overall purpose and objectives of a project.

- **Stakeholder requirements** represent the viewpoints of stakeholders, individuals or groups who have an interest in the outcome of the project by capturing their needs, expectations and concerns.

- **Solution requirements** provide details on how the project will fulfil the business needs and are further divided into two sub-categories:

  - **Functional requirements** detail what the solution should do in terms of specific functionalities, capabilities and behaviours that the system, product or service must possess.

  - **Non-functional requirements** specify qualities, characteristics and conditions for the solution to remain effective, such as performance, usability, scalability and other system attributes.

- **Transition requirements** facilitate transition from the current state to the future state. They are temporary in nature and are not needed when completed.

Cyber security extension
Business analysts can support in:

- Defining business requirements related to the protection of critical assets, compliance related to cyber security regulations and identifying the relevant business goals and objectives for cyber security measures.

- Identifying stakeholders who have a vested interest in the security of the system and their specific requirements by capturing their expectations and concerns related to cyber security.

- Specifying solution requirements for security features and functionalities that contribute to the overall system resilience by implementing controls, access management, encrypting the data, privacy and other security measures.

- Detailing functional requirements related to cyber security features, such as authentication, authorisation, intrusion detection and secure data processing.

- Incorporating non-functional requirements specific to cyber security, such as performance under security load, response times for security incidents and aspects such as system availability, reliability and scalability in the context of cyber security.

- Specifying data requirements related to the protection of sensitive information to ensure the secure handling of data by using encryption, access control and other data integrity requirements and defining metrics for measuring the effectiveness of security controls.

- Explicitly stating assumptions related to cyber security, such as the assumed level of security awareness among users, the trustworthiness of third-party components or the effectiveness of security controls.

Development phase

The predominant activities for business analysts during the development phase are to: collaborate with stakeholders to address questions or concerns raised during development, work closely with the development team to clarify any ambiguities in the requirements and change control management by setting up a process for managing changes and ensuring that changes are evaluated, impact assessed, prioritised, approved, controlled and methodically implemented.

Business analysts can collaborate with system architects and developers to illustrate how end users will interact with the system through use cases and user stories and ensure that those use cases are technically feasible and align with the overall system architecture. They also assist in prioritising requirements based on business value and technical feasibility.

Cyber security extension

During the development phase, which inherently leans towards technical intricacies, supporting system architects and developers can pose a challenge for business analysts who lack technical expertise. Nonetheless, business analysts without a technical background can play a crucial role by posing a strategic set of questions to ensure that cyber security considerations are integrated in the architecture and the code.

Some key questions, and not an exhaustive list, are:

- Are there security measures integrated into the architecture to protect against potential threats and vulnerabilities?

- How is the overall system architecture designed to ensure the confidentiality, integrity and availability of sensitive data?

- How are sensitive data identified and classified within the system architecture?

- What encryption mechanisms and access controls are in place to protect data both in transit and at rest?

- How are user authentication and authorisation managed in the system architecture?
- Are there measures in place to prevent unauthorised access to critical system components?
- Are there security considerations addressed when integrating third-party components or services into the system architecture?
- Are there measures taken to ensure the security of application programming interfaces (APIs) and external interfaces?
- How is the system architecture designed to facilitate a timely and effective response to security incidents?
- What are the key components of the incident response plan within the architecture?
- How does the system architecture align with relevant cyber security regulations and compliance standards?
- What documentation is available to demonstrate adherence to industry-specific security requirements?
- Are there secure coding practices incorporated into the development process?
- Are developers trained on best practices for preventing common security vulnerabilities?
- How is user authentication implemented, and what methods are used to ensure strong password security?
- How are authorisation checks enforced to control user access rights?
- Are there processes in place to regularly update and patch dependencies?
- How are security considerations incorporated into the code review process?
- Is there a focus on identifying and addressing security-related code vulnerabilities?
- What resources and training opportunities are available to developers to stay updated on evolving cyber security threats and best practices?
- How is knowledge sharing encouraged within the development team to enhance overall security awareness?

By posing these questions, business analysts can facilitate a dialogue that ensures cyber security considerations are addressed at both the architectural and implementation levels of the project. This collaboration enables the creation of more secure and resilient systems.

Testing phase

While testing is not the primary focus of the business analyst's role, they do play a significant role in ensuring the quality and effectiveness of the solutions they help to design and implement. The involvement of a business analyst in testing activities varies depending on the organisation, project and specific phase of the project life cycle.

With reference to testing, the BABOK v3 typically addresses aspects related to the verification and validation of solutions during the requirements and implementation phases. It also outlines knowledge areas that are particularly relevant to testing, such as:

- **Requirements analysis and design definition:** BABOK v3 emphasises the importance of validating requirements and designs to ensure that they meet stakeholder needs. Testing is a key activity within this knowledge area to verify that the specified requirements and designs are accurate and aligned with business objectives.

- **Solution evaluation:** This knowledge area involves assessing the performance of implemented solutions. Testing plays a crucial role in this phase to confirm that the solution functions as intended and satisfies the specified requirements. It includes both formal testing processes and user acceptance testing.

- **Underlying competencies:** The underlying competencies section of the BABOK v3 includes skills and knowledge related to communication, analytical thinking and solution assessment and validation. These competencies are essential for effective testing processes, including communication with stakeholders and the ability to analyse and validate the correctness of implemented solutions.

- **Techniques:** Finally, the BABOK v3 introduces various techniques that can be applied during the testing process, such as acceptance and evaluation criteria, and validation. These techniques guide business analysts in ensuring that the delivered solutions meet the defined criteria and address business needs.

Business analysts, as per the BABOK v3, should collaborate with other stakeholders, including testing professionals, to ensure the quality and effectiveness of the solutions being delivered. The goal is to validate that the solutions meet the defined requirements and contribute to achieving the desired business outcomes.

Cyber security extension
Business analysts can support in:

- Performing requirements validation by collaborating with cyber security experts to validate that security requirements are adequately reflected in the overall requirements. Ensure that security controls, data protection measures and compliance requirements are explicitly addressed.

- Testing planning by working closely with cyber security teams to incorporate specific security testing objectives, such as penetration testing, vulnerability assessments and compliance checks, into the overall test plan.

- Supporting test case design by collaborating with cyber security experts to identify and design test cases specifically focused on security aspects. This includes testing for confidentiality, integrity, availability and resilience of the system.

- Performing user acceptance testing (UAT) by working with end users to validate that security features and controls align with their expectations. Educate users on cyber security best practices and gather feedback on the user experience with security measures.

- Supporting defect management activities by helping to prioritise and communicate cyber security-related defects, emphasising the potential impact on data security, compliance and overall system integrity.

- Documenting by collaborating with the cyber security team on the test results and findings. Also, support the documenting of security controls, configurations and any adjustments made during the testing phase.

By incorporating these cyber security considerations into testing activities, business analysts can contribute to building a secure and resilient system that not only meets business requirements but also aligns with the organisation's cyber security objectives. This collaborative approach helps to identify and address security vulnerabilities earlier, thereby shifting the cyber security considerations left in the development life cycle.

SUMMARY

The concept of 'shifting left' in cyber security took centre stage in this chapter, emphasising the strategic integration of security considerations and controls at the early stages of the software development and IT operations life cycle. The primary goal is to proactively address security vulnerabilities and risks, minimising the likelihood of security issues and mitigating their potential impact during later stages.

The chapter underscores the imperative nature of making cyber security an integral part of discussions throughout the entire project life cycle. By advocating for the incorporation of cyber security alongside all other project deliverables, you are setting the stage for a proactive and holistic approach to security. Recognising the unique context of each organisation and project, it emphasises that there is no one-size-fits-all solution to cyber security, or security in general.

To address security vulnerabilities at the earliest stages, this chapter has provided practical pointers aimed at bringing pertinent cyber security conversations to the table during every phase of the project. These pointers serve as guidelines, encouraging a security mindset and the involvement of security expertise at crucial junctures. The overarching aim for a business analyst is asking the right questions at the right time, ensuring that cyber security is not an afterthought but an integral part of the project's DNA.

> The overarching aim for a business analyst is asking the right questions at the right time, ensuring that cyber security is not an afterthought but an integral part of the project's DNA.

The next chapter takes a hard pivot, centring attention back to the Business Analysis and Cyber Security Framework and focusing on securing the crown jewels.

TAKEAWAY QUESTIONS

- What are your key learning points in this chapter?
- What is the one lesson that you'll implement?
- How do you envision incorporating cyber security considerations into your current or future projects, inspired by the insights shared in this chapter?

7 SECURING THE CROWN JEWELS

Here's what you'll learn from this chapter:

- Data – the lifeblood of modern society.
- Too much data.
- Data security vs cyber security.
- The data states.
- Approach to data security.
- Emerging data trends to monitor.

We have broadened the framework in previous chapters, where the foundational mindset and the two pillars of risk analysis and business analysis were established. In this chapter, our focus shifts towards the 'data security' domain, emphasising the imperative of safeguarding the 'crown jewels' (Figure 7.1).

Figure 7.1 Business Analysis and Cyber Security Framework with data security
(Copyright: I-Perceptions Consulting Ltd)

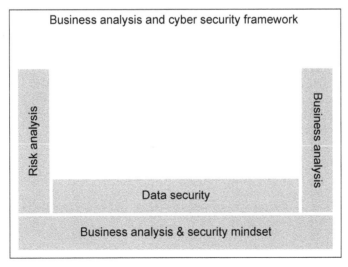

DATA – THE LIFEBLOOD OF MODERN SOCIETY

When I heard the statement 'data is the non-depletable oxygen' (Thoughtspot, 2023) from Geraldine Wong, chief data officer (CDO) of GXS Bank, it got me thinking. From the words we read, the images we see and the conversations we have, to the tactile experiences of touch, everything has seamlessly transformed into data. The very fabric of our existence, once confined to the tangible and ephemeral, is now intricately intertwined with the intangible threads of information. Each interaction, visual, auditory or tactile, leaves a digital footprint, contributing to the vast landscape of data that shape our contemporary reality. In this all-encompassing data ecosystem, the omnipresence of data has our expressions, observations and sensory perceptions converge into a mosaic of information, illustrating the profound and inescapable presence of data in every facet of today's interconnected world.

Much like oxygen is indispensable for sustaining life in the human body, data serve as the lifeblood of our modern, interconnected society. Oxygen, the essential element that enables cellular respiration and energy production, is analogous to the fundamental role that data play in fuelling the processes and functions of various facets of our daily existence.

In the human body, oxygen is distributed through the bloodstream to every organ, ensuring vitality. Similarly, data permeate every aspect of our contemporary lives, encompassing financial transactions, personal interactions, work-related activities and memories.

See the respiratory system as a metaphor for the data infrastructure. The respiratory system extracts oxygen from the air and expels carbon dioxide, facilitating the exchange of gases vital for life. Likewise, our data systems extract valuable insights from the vast data storehouses of information, creating a dynamic exchange that powers decision-making, innovation and societal development.

DATA IS THE NON-DEPLETABLE OXYGEN

Oxygen, the essential element that enables cellular respiration and energy production, is analogous to the fundamental role that data plays in fuelling the processes and functions of various facets of our daily existence.

Just as oxygen is integral to the functioning of individual cells, data are essential for the operation of various sectors, including finance, healthcare, education and commerce. Financial transactions, for instance, are analogous to the respiratory exchange at the cellular level. Each transaction represents a flow of data that sustains the economic health of the system. Similarly, once recorded in physical diaries or photo albums, our memories are now digitised, forming an intricate network of personal data that defines our identity and shapes our experiences.

The analogy extends to the interconnectedness of systems. The respiratory system collaborates with other systems to maintain equilibrium in the human body. Likewise, data are interwoven into the fabric of our society, interacting with technological, economic and social systems to create a complex and interdependent network.

Much like oxygen, which is vital but requires careful regulation to prevent imbalance or toxicity, data must be managed responsibly. Privacy, security and ethical use arises, mirroring the importance of maintaining a delicate balance in the body's oxygen levels.

Data, like the circulatory system, must have mechanisms to protect against contamination or infection and require vigilant protection. In the same way that the body's immune system guards against threats, robust cyber security measures and ethical data management practices are essential shields for safeguarding data. The analogy can also be extended to highlight the importance of maintaining the balance. Just as an imbalance in the body's blood composition can lead to health issues, any compromise in the security or ethical use of data can result in adverse consequences.

In order to harness the power of data for innovation and progress, it becomes necessary to recognise their vulnerability and implement stringent measures to ensure the reliability and safety of our digital lifeblood.

TOO MUCH DATA

Michalis Zinieris, in his insightful article titled 'Data: A Small Four-Letter Word Which Has Grown Exponentially to Such a Big Value' (Zinieris, n.d.), projects a staggering estimate that our global data volume is poised to reach 175 zettabytes by 2025. To put this colossal figure into perspective, imagine a stack of Blu-ray discs extending to the moon 23 times over. Astonishingly, this is merely the nascent stage of data proliferation. Earlier, it was humans who predominantly contributed to the generation of data. However, the landscape has radically shifted, with machines and sensors generating an unprecedented volume of data, primarily propelled by the exponential growth of IoT. This surge in data production poses a formidable challenge, overwhelming organisations and often leaving them paralysed, unsure where to begin their data management endeavours. As the magnitude of data becomes increasingly intricate, grappling with the challenge of understanding it compounds the difficulty of securing it.

Data preparation is intrinsic to ensuring effective data security. Data quality, accuracy and structure are foundational elements that significantly impact the success of security measures and even legal requirements for domains such as healthcare, finance, etc. A meticulous data preparation process involves cleaning, validating and organising data, providing a reliable basis for implementing security protocols. Accurate data are essential for precisely applying security measures, including encryption, access controls and authentication mechanisms. Consistent encoding practices and eliminating redundancies during data preparation contribute to clarity, reducing data structure ambiguity and enhancing the precision of security controls. Moreover, effective data preparation aids in identifying and addressing potential risks and vulnerabilities and mitigating the likelihood of security breaches. The synergy between data preparation and data security is paramount, as the former ensures that security measures operate on a solid foundation of reliable and well-organised information.

DATA SECURITY VS CYBER SECURITY

As defined in Chapter 3, cyber security is 'the protection of systems, networks, applications, processes, people–systems interactions and **data** within the cyberspace'. Data are a subset with specific scope and areas of emphasis within the broader and overarching field of cyber security.

Cyber security extends beyond data protection and overarches to include the overall security of computer systems, networks and the infrastructure that supports them. It involves safeguarding hardware, software and the electronic processes that enable information processing.

Data security is a subset dedicated to safeguarding the confidentiality, integrity and availability of information, thus aligning with the principles of the information security Triad, which is protecting data from unauthorised access, disclosure, alteration or destruction. Data security is concerned with the protection of sensitive and valuable information, regardless of the medium in which it is stored or transmitted. This includes data at rest (stored), data in transit (being transmitted) and data in use (being processed).

Data security measures include encryption, access controls, authentication mechanisms, backup and recovery strategies, and policies governing data handling. There is more on this in the next chapter. The goal is to ensure that only authorised individuals can access data and that they remain unaltered and available when needed.

THE DATA STATES

To understand data security, the organisation's crown jewels, it is fundamental to understand the different data states.

The mere mention of 'crown jewels' instantly transports me back to my visit to the Tower of London, where I was captivated by the sheer grandeur of the sparkling jewels. And whenever 'crown jewels' is used to refer to data, I've found myself consistently drawing parallels between that regal spectacle and the states of data.

The states of data refer to the various conditions or phases that data can exist in throughout their life cycle. Understanding these states of data is crucial for implementing comprehensive data security measures.

Data at rest (stored at the Tower of London)

The Tower of London serves as the primary repository for the Crown Jewels, representing the 'data at rest' phase in the analogy. The secure Jewel House, akin to a fortified data centre, is equipped with advanced security measures to ensure the safety of the treasures while they are not actively in use. The secure storage at the Tower of London aligns with protecting data at rest in secure databases or data centres.

It's worth emphasising that 'data at rest' encompasses various storage environments, including databases, data warehouses, data lakes, cloud storage services, file storage systems and more. These diverse storage options are chosen based on data volume, type, access patterns and performance requirements. Many organisations opt for a strategic combination of these storage solutions to address their diverse data management needs, thereby shaping their customised security measures accordingly.

Data in transit (moving to Buckingham Palace)

When the Crown Jewels need to be transported, a highly orchestrated and secure operation is executed, reflecting the concept of 'data in transit'. The jewels are carefully moved from the Tower of London to Buckingham Palace, drawing parallels with the need for secure data transmission between locations. In this scenario, armoured vehicles and meticulous planning represent the equivalent of encrypted data transfer protocols and secure networks used to move sensitive data. The careful movement of the Crown Jewels parallels the need for secure data transmission protocols when moving sensitive information between locations.

Data in use (worn by the royals)

The pinnacle of the analogy involves the 'data in use' phase, when the Crown Jewels are worn by the royals during ceremonial events. Analogously, organisations must ensure robust security measures are in place when sensitive data are actively used, such as during strategic decision-making, critical business processes or when sharing with suppliers and third parties. This includes secure access controls, encryption during processing and constant monitoring to prevent unauthorised access – equivalent to the vigilance exercised when the royals wear the jewels. The ceremonial use of the Crown Jewels by the royals draws parallels to securing data actively used in business operations, requiring stringent access controls and encryption during processing.

APPROACH TO DATA SECURITY

Now that the scope of data security and cyber security is established, the approach to security will remain the same as cyber security, which is identifying the risks with a security mindset.

In the previous chapters, we discussed how business analysts can extend their analysis to support security and technical teams in addressing cyber security needs. Similarly, below are some of the ways business analysts can collaborate with stakeholders to support data security activities:

- **Requirements elicitation** – business analysts can work closely with business and security stakeholders to elicit and document data security requirements. This involves understanding business processes, identifying sensitive data and determining security needs.

- **Risk analysis and assessment** – business analysts can support security and data teams by conducting risk analysis and assessments related to data security. This includes identifying potential risks to data assets, assessing their impact and proposing mitigation strategies.

- **Data classification** – business analysts can collaborate with stakeholders to classify data based on sensitivity and criticality. Establishing a data classification framework helps to prioritise security measures.

- **Privacy impact assessments (PIAs)** – business analysts can assist data teams in conducting PIAs to evaluate the potential impact of projects on privacy and data protection, ensuring compliance with relevant regulations.

- **Policy and procedure development** – business analysts can work with relevant governance teams to develop and document data security policies and procedures. This involves translating security requirements into actionable guidelines.

- **Data flow diagrams** – business analysts who work in technical teams (can also be called systems analysts) can support data and technical teams by creating data flow diagrams to illustrate how data move within the organisation. This visual representation helps to identify potential security vulnerabilities and points of control.

- **Incident response planning** – business analysts can contribute to the development of incident response plans by defining procedures for detecting, reporting and responding to security incidents related to data breaches.

- **Security awareness training** – business analysts can participate in creating and delivering security awareness training for teams handling sensitive data. This ensures that everyone is aware of their role in maintaining data security.

- **Continuous improvement** – business analysts can engage in continuous improvements by analysing security incidents, lessons learned and feedback, and propose enhancements to security measures based on evolving threats and technology changes.

While business analysts may not possess exhaustive knowledge of data security requirements, given that it falls within the domain of security teams, their analytical skills, effective communication abilities and understanding of business operations allow them to cultivate collaboration between business, governance, IT and security teams. As a bridge between stakeholders, business analysts can play a pivotal role in ensuring that data security considerations are seamlessly integrated into business processes and systems, enhancing the organisation's overall security posture.

Securing the flows

Securing a process flow against cyber security threats and risks, including safeguarding data (at rest, in transit and in use), requires a collaborative and multidisciplinary approach that involves understanding the process, implementing security controls and ensuring compliance. While business analysts may not be cyber security experts, they can play a crucial role in securing the process flows.

Business analysts can collaborate with stakeholders to identify critical assets and sensitive data within the processes and facilitate risk assessments to evaluate potential threats. They can also actively participate in classifying data based on sensitivity and defining appropriate handling procedures, addressing data at rest, in transit and in use.

Business analysts can contribute to securing data transmission by understanding and documenting how data are communicated between different components of the process flow. Collaborating with IT and security teams, business analysts can contribute to implementing access controls, emphasising role-based access and the principle of least privilege for data in use.

Furthermore, business analysts can contribute to incident response planning, documenting procedures for responding to cyber security incidents and defining roles and responsibilities for a coordinated response.

Finally, they can influence fostering a culture of continuous improvement to ensure that security measures within the processes are regularly reviewed and updated based on changes in the business environment and emerging threats.

REFLECTION TIME

Take a moment, ponder and write down:

- How is your organisation protecting customer data, and are there ways to make it even more secure to comply with data protection rules?
- Have you looked into getting valuable insights from all your data, including untapped information, that could improve your decision-making?

EMERGING DATA TRENDS TO MONITOR

Before concluding this chapter, let's explore a few noteworthy data trends that are especially pertinent for business analysts closely collaborating with data, governance and security teams.

Data are the new currency

In his article 'Data is the New Currency. Don't Let It Slip Through Your Fingers', Peter Daisyme underscores data's paramount importance as the primary currency in the digital age, surpassing other technological developments. He highlights the evolution of data's role in businesses, emphasising the untapped potential within dark data. While acknowledging the prevalent focus on high-level data, his article advocates for a more comprehensive approach, stressing the need to handle data correctly from the start. A robust data strategy, including identification, organisation and analysis, is essential. The article recommends leveraging technology, such as data observability applications, to transform unstructured data into valuable insights throughout the organisation. Cultivating a data-driven culture is seen as crucial, and the article concludes by outlining steps for companies to harness the power of data as the currency of the future, emphasising commitment, technology adoption and growth-oriented organisational culture (Daisyme, 2023).

As per Alice Nunwick's article, 'Data to Become New Currency in the Age of AI, Says Analyst' (Nunwick, 2023), in an industry update, GlobalData principal analyst Natasha Rybak asserts that data will be the new currency in the age of AI, emphasising the pivotal role of high-quality datasets for effective AI tools. Rybak contends that businesses aiming to maximise their data's value must make substantial investments in refining and displaying data, requiring significant time, unimpeded access and adherence to legal requirements.

Rybak delves into legal issues and use cases surrounding personal data owned by major businesses such as Meta, Walmart and Sky. Both Sky UK and Walmart utilise personal and behavioural data to personalise customer experiences. Sky UK's Search Behaviour tool, for example, enables precise audience targeting based on metrics such as location and age. However, Rybak notes potential legal challenges, citing Meta's recent troubles with Norway's data protection agency over personalised advertisements. Rybak compares data to 'diamonds in the rough' for businesses implementing AI, a sentiment echoed by others. International Competition Network chair Andreas Bundt warns that AI could reinforce 'Big Tech' dominance due to their extensive data holdings, potentially disadvantaging smaller AI startups. Businesses aiming to leverage AI must recognise the value of their data and navigate the legal considerations associated with their use.

These articles emphasise the critical role of data in the contemporary digital landscape. Peter Daisyme's piece spotlights data as the primary currency, stressing the need for a comprehensive approach to handling it correctly from the beginning, focusing on a robust data strategy, technology adoption and fostering a data-driven organisational culture. Alice Nunwick's article discusses how data will be the new currency in the age of AI, emphasising the importance of high-quality datasets for effective AI tools. The common thread in both articles is the recognition of data as valuable assets and the need for businesses to strategically manage, refine and protect them in the evolving technological landscape.

Through a business analyst's lens, the crux lies in recognising the pivotal role of data in today's digital landscape. Ultimately, a business analyst working closely with data and governance teams should grasp the centrality of data, embrace a holistic approach to their management, stay attuned to legal implications and view data as a strategic asset vital for business resilience.

A data risk framework

Sarah Telford and Stefaan G. Verhulst, in their article 'A Framework For Understanding Data Risk' (Telford and Verhulst, 2016), introduce a comprehensive framework for assessing and managing data risk within organisations, developed in collaboration with the Harvard Humanitarian Initiative. This framework provides a structured approach for organisations to navigate and mitigate data risks throughout the entire data life cycle.

This framework guides organisations through a systematic process, starting with an assessment that scrutinises the context of data generation and sharing, including anticipated benefits and potential threats. The subsequent step involves conducting a detailed data inventory covering storage locations and accessibility. Identifying potential risks and harms, such as data correlation or breaches, prepares staff for various scenarios. The framework concludes with implementing countermeasures, including developing data handling policies, implementing access controls and providing staff training on responsible data use. For business analysts, this systematic and thorough framework offers a valuable tool to navigate and mitigate data risks throughout the entire data life cycle in organisations, aligning with their role in strategically managing, refining and protecting data in the evolving technological landscape.

The Big Data disaster

The study conducted by Sean Martin McDonald with support from the Open Society Foundation, Ford Foundation and Media Democracy Fund, titled 'Ebola: A Big Data Disaster' (McDonald, 2016), explores the use of Big Data, specifically call detail record (CDR) data, in humanitarian crises such as the Ebola outbreak in West Africa. The research emphasises the challenges of digital humanitarian coordination, particularly regarding privacy concerns and the impact on human rights. McDonald focuses on legal frameworks related to privacy and property, questioning the unregulated use of CDRs and highlighting the potential opportunities and risks of applying data science to international development. The paper raises important legal questions about information access, data sharing limitations and privacy invasion proportionality in the context of the public good. It emphasises the need for critical dialogue around the experimental nature of data modelling in emergency responses to safeguard human rights. The study offers a valuable perspective for organisations like the Centre for Internet and Society, advocating for critically examining Big Data's implications for human rights and sustainable development.

From a business analyst's perspective, the study demonstrates the challenges and opportunities in employing large datasets during emergencies, providing insights into the legal frameworks and privacy considerations surrounding data use. It emphasises ethical concerns related to experimenting with humanitarian technologies and their impact on privacy, which is crucial for business analysts involved in data-driven projects. The analysis of risks associated with using CDRs without user consent informs business analysts engaged in risk assessment and management, particularly in fields such as public health or crisis response. Understanding the implications of Big Data on human rights and sustainable development is essential for socially responsible business practices, broadening the analyst's perspective on the ethical dimensions of data usage. Lastly, the article calls for critical discussions on the experimental nature of data modelling in emergency responses, urging business analysts to engage in conversations around responsible data use and its potential impact on human rights within their organisations.

In essence, these emerging data trends accentuate the imperative for organisations to adopt strategic, ethical and comprehensive approaches to data management. Understanding and navigating the challenges and opportunities associated with data can become vital aspects of a business analyst's role in the evolving digital landscape.

SUMMARY

The chapter has delved into the critical topic of data security, recognising data as the lifeblood of modern society. It navigated through key facets such as the distinction between data security and cyber security. The chapter elucidated the significance of understanding the three data states for crafting effective data security strategies tailored to specific situations. It explored strategies to ensure the safe passage of data throughout their life cycle, considering the various touchpoints and potential vulnerabilities within the flow.

Showcasing the dynamic nature of the data landscape, the chapter discussed emerging data trends to monitor, offering diverse perspectives on the contemporary challenges and opportunities associated with managing and securing data.

The next chapter further advances the construction of the Business Analysis and Cyber Security Framework, delving into the next dimension: people and personas.

TAKEAWAY QUESTIONS

- What are your key learning points in this chapter?
- What is the one lesson that you'll implement?
- How do you summarise your perspectives on data security?

8   MASQUERADES

Here's what you'll learn from this chapter:

- People management.
- Personas.
- Misuse cases.
- Incident management.
- Business continuity plan.
- Components of the business continuity plan.

THE WEAK LINK

We established in the previous chapters that people are the weakest link, and managing them is pivotal in cyber security. Human errors, unintentional or deliberate, contribute to a substantial portion of cyber security breaches.

> As reported by the BBC, Egor Igorevich Kriuchkov, a Russian man in the USA, pleaded guilty to attempting to extort money from Tesla by plotting a ransomware attack on the company's battery plant in Nevada. Kriuchkov, acting on behalf of criminals, allegedly offered an employee $1 million to carry out the attack and steal company secrets (BBC, 2021). The FBI and Tesla thwarted the planned attack, and Kriuchkov faced up to 10 months in prison after pleading guilty. He mentioned the Russian government's awareness of the plot, but there are no allegations of ties to the Kremlin.

This incident highlights the significance of employee awareness and collaboration in preventing cyber threats. In this case, the Tesla employee targeted by the extortion attempt played a crucial role by reporting the plot to the company and cooperating with the FBI. This underscores the importance of having well-informed and vigilant employees as a part of effective people management in cyber security to recognise and mitigate potential threats.

As cited in an article in *Infosecurity Magazine*, a social experiment conducted by the IT industry association CompTIA revealed alarming insights into security awareness (Seals, 2015). Between August and October 2015, 200 unbranded USB sticks were strategically placed in high-traffic public spaces across major US cities. Shockingly, 18 per cent of those who found the USB drives plugged them into their devices, opened the text files, clicked on unique links or emailed the listed address, potentially exposing their devices and information to cyber security risks. Millennials were found to be more susceptible, with 40 per cent likely to pick up a USB stick, compared to 22 per cent of Gen X and 9 per cent of Baby Boomers (Seals, 2015). Again, the experiment underscores the need for increased security awareness, proactive IT security measures and ongoing training for employees to mitigate cyber security risks. CompTIA emphasised the crucial role that vendors can play in educating clients, implementing security solutions and fostering a culture of cyber security within organisations. The survey also highlighted concerns about poor password protection, use of public Wi-Fi networks and inadequate cyber security training practices among employees, emphasising the need for continuous and comprehensive security initiatives.

Although an effective people management strategy involves comprehensive training programmes to educate employees on security protocols, identify potential threats and instil best practices, human errors cannot be avoided.

HUMAN ERRORS

Human errors generally refer to mistakes, oversights or unintended actions made by individuals that deviate from the intended course of action or expectations. These errors can occur in various aspects of life and work, leading to undesired outcomes. Some examples of human errors include forgetfulness, lapses in attention, misinterpretation of information, misjudgement and failure to follow established procedures. Human errors are inherent to human nature and various factors contribute to their occurrence, including cognitive limitations, environmental conditions and situational complexities. Humans may make mistakes due to factors such as fatigue, stress, distraction or simply the complexity of certain tasks. However, in domains such as healthcare, aviation or cyber security, the consequences of human errors can range from minor inconveniences to severe incidents.

While efforts can be made to reduce the likelihood and impact of errors through training, process improvements and technological aids, achieving 100 per cent avoidance of human error is practically impossible. There will always be some residual risk associated with human error.

Therefore, acknowledging the inevitability of human errors is crucial for developing resilient systems that can detect, recover from and adapt to unexpected situations. Organisations can then implement strategies to mitigate the impact of human errors, such as redundancy in critical systems, error-proofing processes and fostering a culture of continuous improvement and learning.

Understanding human errors is crucial for designing systems and processes that account for the inherent fallibility of individuals and aim to minimise the likelihood and impact of such mistakes.

Additionally, identifying personas based on cyber awareness aids in designing user-friendly security measures, considering the diverse ways individuals interact with technology and perceive security practices.

PERSONAS

Advancing the Business Analysis and Cyber Security Framework (Figure 8.1), this section will delve into the dimension of 'people and personas', and we will explore the 'incident management' and 'business continuity' dimensions of the framework later in the chapter.

Figure 8.1 Business Analysis and Cyber Security Framework with people and personas, incident management and business continuity (Copyright: I-Perceptions Consulting Ltd)

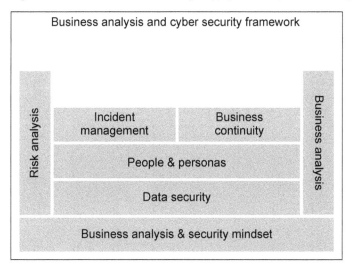

Technique 61 in the third edition of *Business Analysis Techniques* (Cadle et al., 2021), meticulously outlines the process of crafting user personas with examples. Developing personas involves gathering insights through user interviews, surveys and observations and creating detailed character profiles that encapsulate each user type's typical traits, goals and challenges. These personas serve as valuable tools for human-centred design, ensuring that cyber security strategies and technologies align with the diverse needs of end users. Some of the cyber security personas can include:

- **The cautious user** – represents individuals who are generally aware of cyber security risks. They follow best practices, update software promptly and use strong, unique passwords. For example, an accountant or finance team member who manages financial records and transactions emphasises the importance of securing sensitive financial data.

- **The unaware user** – represents users who may lack awareness of potential threats. They may engage in risky online behaviour, such as clicking on suspicious links, and require additional education. For example, an administrative assistant who handles routine administrative tasks may have limited awareness of cyber security risks.

- **The tech-savvy professional** – represents users with a strong understanding of technology. They may have specific security needs related to their profession and prefer advanced security features. For example, an IT consultant who works in the IT industry possesses advanced technical knowledge and has specific security needs related to consulting services.

- **The remote worker** – represents individuals who frequently work outside traditional office settings, highlighting unique cyber security considerations for this group. For example, a remote marketing executive who executes marketing campaigns and works remotely requires secure access to company systems from various locations. With the rise of remote work, this could be necessary for any individual in the organisation.

- **The busy executive** – represents executives who often have distinct security concerns due to their access to sensitive information. This persona helps tailor security measures to meet their specific needs and priorities. For example, the chief executive officer (CEO) who leads the organisation has access to sensitive strategic information and requires robust security measures due to the executive role.

These role examples help to illustrate how personas can be tailored to specific professions, reflecting diverse responsibilities and security considerations within an organisation. Each persona represents a distinct user type, allowing cyber security strategies to address the unique challenges and requirements associated with different roles.

In addition, it is vital to be aware of the personas that could unintentionally pose cyber security risks, such as:

- **The unintentional insider threat** has access to sensitive data but might accidentally expose it through improper handling, sharing or storage practices.

- **The bring-your-own-device (BYOD) user** who uses personal devices for work potentially introduces security risks if these devices are not properly secured or monitored.

- **The social sharer** who shares work-related information on social media without realising the potential impact on cyber security and inadvertently leaks sensitive details.

- **The forgetful employee** who may forget the password and write it down, visible to everyone, or forget to update passwords or follow secure password practices.

- **The uninformed executive** who is unaware of the latest cyber security threats and best practices and may unintentionally make decisions that compromise security.

The above personas highlight individuals who, without malicious intent, can inadvertently compromise cyber security. However, there could be those with malicious intent that the organisation must defend against, so understanding their motivations and methods is crucial for developing effective cyber security measures:

- **The insider threat** is an employee with access privileges intentionally seeking to harm the organisation, possibly for personal gain or revenge.

- **The external hacker** is a cybercriminal, an external threat actor attempting to breach the organisation's systems for financial gain, data theft or other malicious purposes.

- **The nation-state actor** is an operative backed by a nation-state engaging in cyber espionage or sabotage for political, economic or military motives.

- **The script kiddie** is an amateur hacker without deep technical understanding using pre-written scripts or tools to exploit vulnerabilities to create chaos or simply engage in malicious activities for fun or to seek a thrill.

- **The cyber extortionist** is a ransomware operator who initiates attacks to encrypt or block access to data, demanding payment in exchange for restoring access.

- **The malicious dark web user** is an illicit marketplace participant who engages in the trade of stolen data, exploits or cybercrime services on the dark web. The dark web is a part of the internet that is intentionally hidden and inaccessible through standard web browsers and requires specific software and configurations to access, and it is intentionally designed to provide anonymity to users.

- **The hacktivist** is an activist hacker who hacks systems to promote a social or political agenda, often through defacement or disruption.

- **The cyber mercenary** is a freelance hacker hired to perform cyber attacks on behalf of individuals, organisations or even nation-states.

Business analysts often create personas as part of their analysis, which are detailed representations of fictional characters, each embodying a specific user type or stakeholder group. These personas help business analysts to understand the diverse needs, goals and behaviours of the end users or stakeholders involved in a project. By creating personas, business analysts can ensure that the developed solutions align with the expectations and requirements of the target audience.

In the context of cyber security, personas can be extended to include security-related characteristics. Business analysts can define the security personas listed above to represent different user roles and their associated security requirements, behaviours and potential threats.

By incorporating security personas into their analysis, business analysts contribute to a more comprehensive understanding of the system's security requirements. This, in turn, helps in developing solutions that not only meet functional expectations but also address security concerns effectively. Personas serve as valuable tools for communication and collaboration among cross-functional teams, ensuring a shared understanding of user needs and security considerations throughout the project life cycle.

Mitigating cyber security risks involves addressing both inside and external threat actors with tailored access-control measures, such as authorisation and authentication protocols, coupled with vigilant monitoring of employee activities through auditing. Nurturing a security-conscious culture is equally essential and achievable through comprehensive training programmes that educate employees on security protocols.

These measures collectively help organisations to safeguard against potential threats posed by employees, whether intentional or unintentional, thereby fortifying their cyber security defences.

Moreover, effective people management extends to incident response, ensuring organisations maintain clear communication channels, well-defined roles and a trained workforce capable of swift and effective responses to security incidents – an aspect detailed later in this chapter.

MISUSE CASES

Along with the personas, business analysts can develop misuse cases in parallel with use cases. Misuse cases focus on how threat actors could intentionally compromise or misuse the system. While business analysts may not possess deep technical expertise, they can actively engage in addressing cyber security concerns through collaboration, communication and leveraging available resources. They can extract valuable insights into how threat actors might intentionally compromise or misuse the system. Collaborative efforts with security professionals enable business analysts to capture misuse scenarios that may not be immediately apparent during traditional requirements gathering. For instance, a misuse case in an online banking system could be an attacker attempting to perform unauthorised transactions by exploiting weak authentication mechanisms.

Business analysts can translate threat scenarios into security user stories. For example, in a healthcare application, a security user story might involve encrypting sensitive patient data to prevent unauthorised access by malicious insiders. In translating technical details into business requirements, they can ensure alignment with organisational objectives.

By engaging with cyber security experts, business analysts can understand threat scenarios and incorporate those scenarios in their impact analysis and help to prioritise countermeasures. For instance, in a smart home automation system, security experts might highlight a threat scenario where attackers exploit insecure IoT devices to gain control over home appliances.

Through consistent collaboration with business, security and IT teams, business analysts can contribute to ensuring a more robust identification and mitigation of threat scenarios in use or misuse cases.

REFLECTION TIME

Take a moment, ponder and write down:

- Can you recall instances from your own experience where human errors led to cyber security vulnerabilities or incidents within your personal life or in your organisation?

- How confident are you in your organisation's ability to manage cyber security risks associated with remote working?

GRACEFULLY RESPONDING AND SEAMLESSLY TRANSITIONING

The legend about bamboo I have heard is that when a seedling is planted, the first year seems uneventful despite providing the necessary sunlight, water and nutrients. Years two, three and four echo a similar quiet growth. However, the magic happens in the fifth year, when the sprig rapidly ascends, reaching an impressive height of 90 ft within five weeks (Sergeyev, 2021).

Contrary to appearances, the initial four years are a crucial phase when bamboo invests its energy in downward growth. Unseen to the eye, it extends its roots deep into the ground, establishing a robust foundation that ultimately supports its towering stature. The bamboo's ability to grow tall lies in its earlier focus on strengthening its roots below the surface.

Another remarkable thing about bamboo is that it exhibits extraordinary strength, standing resilient against powerful winds that might topple other trees. It is a testament to its outstanding endurance, having survived even atom bombs and natural disasters (Gilmer, n.d.). In the face of forceful winds, bamboo displays a unique flexibility: it gracefully bends with the force of the wind and promptly returns upright once the wind subsides. This inherent resilience, strength and adaptability in the face of adversity makes bamboo a symbol of resilience (Sergeyev, 2021).

The dictionary meaning of resilience is the capacity to recover quickly from difficulties or the ability of a substance or object to spring back into shape. It's the toughness and the elasticity.

As the saying goes, you cannot direct the wind, but you can adjust your sails. In a similar vein, threats cannot be entirely avoided, yet they can be anticipated and mitigated through careful preparation and planning. Despite dedicated efforts involving controls, measures, process enhancements, training and technological support, it remains impractical to eliminate every risk and thwart every threat. However, with meticulous prior planning, organisations can effectively manage risks and threats. Resilience is paramount for organisations, and preparation is the bedrock of this resilience, allowing them to navigate the unpredictable waters of potential disruptions.

Preparedness involves adeptly responding to the inevitable and gracefully managing incidents as they unfold. Seamlessly transitioning from the impact of a disaster to resuming regular business operations, all achieved through meticulous prior planning and preparation, defines the essence of business continuity.

> Preparedness involves adeptly responding to the inevitable and gracefully managing incidents as they unfold.

INCIDENT MANAGEMENT

Incident management is the structured process of identifying, responding to and resolving incidents or disruptions in an organisation's operations. These incidents can range from cyber security breaches and IT system failures to natural disasters and other emergencies. The goal of incident management is to respond efficiently by minimising the impact of disruptions, restoring normal operations swiftly and learning from the incident to prevent future occurrences. The process typically involves **detection**, **reporting**, **assessment**, **classification**, **response**, **resolution** and **post-incident** analysis.

Business analyst support

While business analysts may not possess all the technical details related to cyber security or incident response, their ability to understand business processes, facilitate communication between different teams and focus on the business impact of incidents makes them valuable contributors to incident management planning and execution.

Business analysts can employ various skills to contribute effectively, such as communication skills to articulate incident management processes clearly to technical and non-technical stakeholders. They can engage stakeholders from different departments to elicit incident response requirements, including understanding the critical business processes, dependencies and potential risks.

They can harness their analytical skills by analysing incident data, identifying patterns and deriving insights for process improvement. Their facilitation skills are essential for discussions and tabletop exercises (simulated scenario-based training exercises that allow participants to review and discuss their organisation's response procedures for various emergency situations or critical incidents in a low-stress environment) involving business and technical teams.

Problem-solving skills are valuable in resolving business-related challenges during incidents, contributing to effective incident response. Additionally, strong documentation skills are necessary to create comprehensive documentation for incident management plans, procedures and post-incident reports.

Business analysts' expertise in various tools can support incident management planning and preparation activities. Collaboration tools such as Confluence or SharePoint help to create centralised repositories for incident management documentation and communication plans. Project management tools such as Jira or Azure Dev Ops aid in tracking and managing incident response tasks and timelines. Visualisation tools such as Lucidchart or Visio assist in creating process flowcharts and visual representations of incident management workflows. Training and learning platforms can be employed to develop and deliver training materials related to incident response.

In addition, business analysts can apply different techniques to enhance incident management processes. SWOT analysis helps to assess the strengths and weaknesses of the current incident management process and identify improvement opportunities. Root cause analysis investigates incidents, identifies root causes and recommends corrective actions.

Scenario planning allows for anticipation of potential incidents and developing response strategies through scenario-based planning. User stories and use cases effectively capture and document business requirements for incident response processes. Lessons-learned workshops facilitate discussions after incidents, gather feedback and identify areas for improvement.

By using these skills, tools and techniques, business analysts can actively participate in incident management planning, execution and continuous improvement efforts. Their unique ability to bridge the gap between business needs and technical requirements can prove crucial in building the organisation's resilience capabilities.

BUSINESS CONTINUITY PLANNING

BCP is a proactive approach that organisations adopt to ensure the continuation of critical business functions in the face of disruptive events such as natural disasters, existential threats, pandemics, cyber security incidents or any other emergencies. The goal of BCP is to minimise the impact of disruptions, maintain essential operations and swiftly recover to normality.

A BCP is a strategic document detailing how an organisation will navigate and recover from disruptions, encompassing tasks such as maintaining customer service, sustaining regular operations and prioritising safety measures. It's crucial to note that a BCP is dynamic, requiring regular reviews and updates to align with organisational changes, be it in facilities, processes or technology.

As highlighted in Chapter 4, in a podcast episode from McKinsey's 'Inside the Strategy Room' (Aufreiter et al., 2022), Nora Aufreiter, Celia Huber and Ophelia Usher shared a board perspective on ensuring readiness for existential risks, and one of the activities they suggested was to prepare a well-balanced business resilience plan focusing on all dimensions, including financial, operational, technical, resources, reputation and business models, and prioritise the scenarios, allocating budget and resources to those and creating processes for managing incidents and business continuity.

A well-crafted BCP is integral to organisational resilience, delivering crucial benefits. First and foremost, it ensures stakeholder safety by providing clear guidelines for emergency response and safeguarding employees, customers and other vital entities.

Furthermore, it acts as a shield for the organisation's reputation, as the rapid and efficient responses outlined in the plan showcase its adept crisis management capabilities. Equally significant is the BCP's role in mitigating the financial impact of emergencies through strategic planning, providing a valuable buffer against potential losses. In essence, a healthy BCP proactively fortifies an organisation, empowering it to navigate challenges, protect its people and sustain operational excellence despite unforeseen disruptions.

Business analyst support

Here again, business analysts can use their communication, analytical and documentation skills and various techniques and tools to support every phase of BCP. Their ability to understand business processes and technological aspects positions them as valuable contributors to building resilient and adaptive organisations.

COMPONENTS OF BCP

Business impact analysis

In conducting the business impact analysis (BIA), business analysts can work closely with stakeholders to evaluate the potential impact of disruptions on various business processes. Leveraging tools such as surveys, interviews and data modelling techniques, business analysts can gather crucial information. Visualisation tools such as data flow diagrams assist in mapping out process dependencies to enable decision-making.

Risk assessment

Business analysts can support this by identifying and analysing potential risks. Utilising tools such as SWOT and PESTLE analysis, they can assess the organisation's internal and external threats. They can also be integral in evaluating and prioritising risks and ensuring stakeholders thoroughly understand potential disruptions.

Recovery strategies

As organisations consider different recovery strategies, business analysts can contribute by evaluating these options. They can assist stakeholders in selecting the most effective recovery strategies based on cost, feasibility and impact. Decision matrices and cost–benefit analysis tools can be employed by business analysts to facilitate the decision-making process, ensuring alignment with business objectives.

Plan development

Business analysts can collaborate with stakeholders in translating chosen recovery strategies into detailed plans. Throughout the plan development, business analysts can ensure clarity, alignment with business objectives and integration with existing processes.

Training and awareness

In the implementation phase, business anlysts can contribute by developing training programmes and raising awareness about the BCP, and helping employees to understand their roles and responsibilities in case of disruptions.

Testing and exercises

Business analysts can actively participate in designing and conducting testing scenarios and exercises to evaluate the effectiveness of the BCP. Simulation tools, tabletop exercises and post-exercise evaluation forms can be employed to enhance testing and assessment. Business analysts can also analyse results and recommend improvements, contributing to the ongoing enhancement of the BCP.

Maintenance and review

In the maintenance phase, business analysts can play a crucial role in regularly reviewing and upkeeping the BCP. They can ensure alignment with organisational changes and engage in continuous improvement efforts. Leveraging change management tools, periodic reviews and feedback mechanisms, business analysts can contribute to maintaining an up-to-date and effective BCP that evolves with the dynamic business environment.

Consistent with the prevailing trend in this book to convey messages through storytelling, this chapter wraps up with a narrative, paving the way for the exploration of the final aspects of the framework in the following chapters.

Storytime

Once upon a time, on a seacoast, lived a farmer. He consistently sought help during the fierce winds, but no one was willing to help. All potential helpers were scarce, deterred by the fearsome winds wreaking havoc on crops and homes.

Then, one day a middle-aged man stepped forward, willing to work. During the interview, the farmer inquired about the man's approach to the rough winds, and to his surprise the man calmly asserted that he could sleep when the wind blew. Despite his scepticism, with no one else to help, the farmer reluctantly offered him the job.

The man proved to be a diligent worker, toiling from dawn till dusk, and the farmer found satisfaction in his efforts. However, one fateful night, as the wind howled vehemently, the farmer woke up alarmed and rushed to the farm. To his dismay, he found the man peacefully asleep. Enraged, the farmer woke him, demanding urgent action to secure things before they were swept away. Unfazed, the man, still in bed, insisted 'No sir, I told you I can sleep when the wind blows', and resumed his slumber.

Driven by frustration, the farmer took matters into his own hands, only to discover a well-prepared scene. The haystack was shielded with tarpaulins, the livestock was safely housed within the barn and shutters were securely closed. Everything was meticulously tied down, impervious to the powerful winds. The farmer then realised that the man had pre-emptively prepared everything, allowing him to sleep undisturbed during the storm. Revelation dawned upon the farmer – anticipating the inevitable winds and preparing in advance was the key to a peaceful sleep, unburdened by the anxieties of last-minute chaos.

The story underscores the significance of preparedness, proactive planning, well-defined incident management and business continuity strategy. Just as the middle-aged man was able to sleep soundly amidst the storm, organisations with robust cyber security practices can navigate the challenges of cyber threats with greater resilience and readiness.

The story also emphasises the reality that incidents cannot be entirely avoided. Just as the winds are inevitable, threats are an inherent part of the digital landscape, and organisations must acknowledge this reality. The goal is not just to weather the storm but to emerge stronger by learning from incidents and improving the organisation's cyber security posture.

Anticipating the inevitable winds and preparing in advance was the key to a peaceful sleep, unburdened by the anxieties of last-minute chaos.

Just as the winds are inevitable, threats are an inherent part of the digital landscape, and organisations must acknowledge this reality.

The goal is not just to weather the storm but to emerge stronger by learning from incidents and improving the organisation's cyber security posture.

REFLECTION TIME

Take a moment, ponder and write down:

- How well-prepared is your organisation to respond to cyber security incidents?
- Are there measures in place to mitigate the potential risks associated with external entities?

SUMMARY

This chapter delved into three critical components: people and personas, incident management, and business continuity. It underscored the significance of human factors by illustrating real-life incidents and social experiments, acknowledging the inevitability of human errors. The chapter also introduced a list of cybersecurity-related personas to ensure alignment between cybersecurity strategies, technologies and the diverse needs of end users.

Moreover, it emphasised the role of business analysts in developing misuse cases to anticipate how threat actors might intentionally compromise or misuse systems, thereby translating threat scenarios into actionable security user stories.

Transitioning to incident management and business continuity, the chapter employed the analogy of bamboo to illustrate the process of building business resilience. It stressed the importance of responding gracefully and seamlessly to incidents, akin to the flexibility of bamboo in the face of adverse conditions.

Concluding with the metaphor of a farmer battling harsh winds, the chapter emphasised the inevitability of threats in the digital landscape. It urged organisations to acknowledge this reality, prepare proactively and emerge stronger by learning from incidents to enhance their cyber security posture.

TAKEAWAY QUESTIONS

- What are your key learning points in this chapter?
- What is the one lesson that you'll implement?
- How do you keep employees informed about evolving threats?

9 THE GUARDIANS

Here's what you'll learn from this chapter:

- A 'good' business case.
- Cyber security business case.
- Challenges with cyber security business case.
- Business outcomes.
- Art of negotiation.
- Cyber security policy.
- Components of cyber security policy.

This chapter will focus on 'security policy' and 'business case' aspects of the Business Analysis and Cyber Security Framework (Figure 9.1).

Figure 9.1 Business Analysis and Cyber Security Framework with security policy and business case (Copyright: I-Perceptions Consulting Ltd)

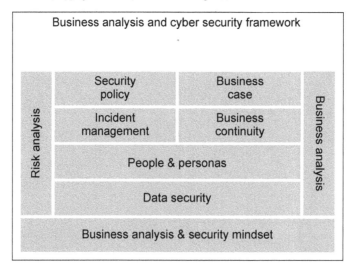

The cyber security business case and the cyber security policy can act as the guardians of cyber resilience by collectively shaping and fortifying an organisation's ability to withstand and recover from cyber threats. The cyber security business case, when meticulously crafted, serves as the strategic blueprint for cyber security investments. The cyber security policy plays a crucial role in setting the guidelines, standards and procedures that govern cyber security practices within the organisation. It establishes a framework for secure operations, defining the rules for data protection, access controls, incident response and other critical aspects of cyber security.

As guardians, they both provide a structured, strategic and proactive approach to cyber security through their combined efforts by fortifying the organisation's defences, enabling it to navigate the complex and ever-changing landscape of cyber threats with resilience and agility.

A 'GOOD' BUSINESS CASE

In my early days as a business analyst, I received valuable advice emphasising that a truly 'good' business case should eloquently answer the pivotal question: 'What's in it for the decision-maker?' This guidance underscored the importance of crafting a compelling case that clearly outlines the specific benefits and advantages the decision-maker stands to gain by approving the proposed project or initiative. This perspective prioritises aligning the project with the approver's interests and objectives and recognises the significance of tailoring the narrative to resonate with their individual motivations and goals. After all, the organisation's goals are intricately woven into the fabric of individual motivations and aspirations.

Securing approval for a business case presents numerous challenges, often rooted in factors such as unclear objectives, insufficient data and unrealistic expectations. In addition, incomplete data and analysis can undermine the credibility of the business case, causing hesitation among approvers.

Furthermore, intangible aspects often involve elements that are challenging to quantify or measure directly in financial terms. These can include factors such as brand reputation, employee morale, customer satisfaction and organisational culture. While these aspects are crucial for overall business success, decision-makers may encounter several challenges when evaluating and prioritising them within a business case.

CYBER SECURITY BUSINESS CASE

Like a standard business case, a typical cyber security business case encompasses essential components crucial for justifying and implementing robust security measures within an organisation.

The executive summary and introduction serve as the gateway, briefly presenting the current cyber security landscape, organisational vulnerabilities and the proposed initiatives. It strategically outlines the objectives and scope, aligning cyber security efforts with broader organisational goals. By defining clear outcomes and specifying the focus areas, stakeholders comprehensively understand the business case's strategic relevance.

Further components include a meticulous risk assessment and consideration of legal and regulatory compliance, emphasising identifying and mitigating potential threats.

The costs and budgeting section provides a transparent breakdown of financial requirements, enabling decision-makers to assess the feasibility of the proposed cyber security enhancements.

Articulating the anticipated return on investment and benefits reinforces the business case's value proposition, emphasising the positive impact on incident reduction, cost savings and organisational reputation. The implementation plan and timeline provide a practical roadmap detailing phased deployment strategies and key milestones for effective integration.

The level of understanding of cyber security among business leaders varies, and it is essential to tailor communication to bridge potential gaps in knowledge. While some leaders may possess a strong grasp of cyber security concepts, others might find the technical intricacies challenging. Effective communication becomes paramount to securing approval for a cyber security business case. Presenting cyber security aspects in a clear, non-technical manner, emphasising the strategic relevance and potential business impacts, is crucial.

Demonstrating how cyber security aligns with overarching business objectives contributes to risk management and provides a clear return on investment, enhancing the likelihood of approval.

Presenting real-world case studies and leveraging external cyber security expertise further aid in conveying the importance of cyber security measures. Ultimately, aligning the narrative with business leaders' priorities ensures a more informed decision-making process and fosters support for cyber security initiatives.

A conventional business case essentially presents a comprehensive overview of a proposed project or initiative. This involves outlining anticipated benefits, projecting return on investment and ensuring alignment with the organisation's broader strategic objectives.

Conversely, a cyber security business case takes a targeted approach to address and mitigate the specific risks associated with the digital landscape. It extensively explores the protection of digital assets, the prevention of security incidents and the overall enhancement of the organisation's security posture. It explicitly outlines the costs of implementing cyber security measures, covering expenses related to security software, hardware, training programmes and cyber security personnel. It emphasises compliance with cyber security regulations, acknowledging the legal requirements and potential financial and reputational risks.

Beyond the tangible costs, the cyber security business case recognises the intangible aspects such as brand reputation and customer trust as paramount considerations. It spotlights the importance of employee training and awareness campaigns to fortify the organisation's resilience against cyber threats, recognising their intangible value to overall cyber security posture.

Business analyst support

As consistently mentioned in previous chapters, here again, business analysts can support cyber security business cases without being cyber security experts by collaborating with security, governance and IT teams. They act as a communication bridge, translating complex technical details into understandable language making the business case accessible to decision-makers without deep technical knowledge. While eliciting requirements, they can ensure that the proposed cyber security measures align with organisational needs.

Business analysts can contribute to risk identification workshops, providing valuable input to the risk assessment section of the business case. They also stay informed about industry regulations, assisting in aligning proposed cyber security measures with regulatory requirements and articulating compliance benefits in the business case. By collaborating with financial experts, business analysts can contribute to cost–benefit analyses, offering insights into potential benefits related to risk reduction, incident prevention and long-term cost savings.

In addition to their role as liaisons between technical and non-technical stakeholders, business analysts can actively contribute to the implementation plan by providing insights into dependencies and constraints, ensuring a realistic approach to deploying cyber security initiatives.

In essence, business analysts can help the development of cyber security business cases by leveraging their analytical and facilitation skills to align proposed measures with organisational objectives.

EFFECTIVE BUSINESS CASES

In his article 'The Business Case: How to Construct a Compelling Argument for Security Initiatives' (2020), Christian Hyatt proposes the six foundational principles for effectively engaging executive decision-makers.

1. **Start with the bottom-line up front (BLUF):** Begin with a concise definition of the problem, a clear request from leadership and expected positive business outcomes. The BLUF should include an executive problem statement, a clear request to leadership and expected benefits.

2. **Clearly articulate 'why we need this':** Define the current programme's shortcomings and the desired future state to explain the necessity of the proposed solution. Quantify the problem without blame and provide evidence for assertions in a detailed appendix.

3. **Build a cost–benefit analysis that leaves no doubt:** Develop a cost–benefit analysis to validate the request. Summarise costs, outline benefits in terms of cost savings or risk management and clearly articulate the ROI. If applicable, align the analysis with the organisation's formal capital project request process.

4. **Include an appendix with additional detail that anticipates questions:** The business case should have an appendix providing detailed supporting information, anticipating potential questions from executives. Include researched sources' comprehensive details, and acknowledge any downsides to prove the authenticity of the business case.

5. **Validate assumptions and socialise the business case before presentation:** Continually validate assumptions by seeking input from other business leaders and collaborating with internal stakeholders throughout the process. Socialise the business case to build advocates and prevent surprises during formal presentations.

6. **Move decision-making forward when momentum stalls:** If faced with non-decision or hesitation, ask for additional details required for a decision and identify factors outside your visibility. Get a commitment on the next steps and follow up regularly to prevent deprioritisation (Hyatt, 2020).

Hyatt asserts that a compelling business case serves several essential functions. First, it is a genuine evaluation of a security initiative's business value, including determining if the investment cannot be sufficiently justified. It validates alignment with business goals and real problem-solving. The business case must clearly communicate and drive timely decision-making on the proposal for non-technical leaders.

In addition, he also states that the business case is not about politicking for personal interests or relying on cyber security fear mongering if underlying business merits are lacking. Leaders must ethically serve the organisation's best interests with intellectual honesty – even willingness to disqualify their own proposals if inadequate business justification exists. Validation of value and return on investment takes priority over self-interest or taking advantage of leadership knowledge gaps.

> The business case is not about politicking for personal interests or relying on cyber security fear mongering if underlying business merits are lacking.
>
> Validation of value and return on investment takes priority over self-interest or taking advantage of leadership knowledge gaps.

CHALLENGES WITH CYBER SECURITY BUSINESS CASES

Business outcomes

Business outcomes in a business case are articulated through business benefits and value. They provide a comprehensive lens through which the success and impact of a project can be assessed.

Benefits represent the tangible and measurable improvements a proposed initiative is expected to deliver, offering a clear picture of the positive changes in specific metrics or outcomes. Benefits can be intangible, too; for example, reduction in a risk of reputational damage is intangible and can't be measured but is still a significant benefit.

Value transcends the numerically quantifiable range, encapsulating the broader worth and significance of the initiative.

The complexity arises from the need to identify and quantify tangible outcomes (benefits) and capture the broader and often intangible aspects that contribute to the overall value of the proposed initiative. However, the complexity in articulating benefits and value is heightened in a cyber security business case. Unlike conventional business cases, cyber security initiatives often involve intangible security aspects, such as risk mitigation, reputation protection and avoiding potential financial losses due to cyber threats. These intangibles are challenging to quantify precisely, yet they constitute a critical part of the overall value proposition.

Additionally, conveying the urgency of cyber security measures and the potentially catastrophic consequences of neglecting them adds an extra layer of complexity. Thus, the cyber security business case demands a delicate balance of tangible and intangible elements, requiring a nuanced approach to effectively communicate the multifaceted value it brings to the organisation.

Below are some of these complexities, among others:

- **Dynamic threat landscape:** The cyber security landscape is dynamic and ever-evolving, making it challenging to accurately predict all potential threats and their corresponding impacts. This uncertainty makes it difficult to provide precise estimates of the benefits associated with cyber security measures.

- **Strategic alignment:** Demonstrating how cyber security initiatives align with broader organisational strategies and contribute to achieving business objectives adds another layer of complexity. Balancing the strategic value of cyber security with its immediate, tangible benefits requires a nuanced approach. Cyber security's long-term, overarching strategic value must be considered, along with addressing the immediate, tangible benefits that stakeholders, especially decision-makers, can understand and appreciate. The long-term factors are enhanced resilience against evolving cyber threats, protection of brand reputation and the establishment of a robust security posture, while the immediate quantifiable advantages include compliance with regulatory standards and safeguarding sensitive data, among others.

- **Organisational perception:** Convincing stakeholders of the value of cyber security measures might be challenging if there's a perception that these initiatives primarily involve costs without clear returns. Overcoming this perception requires effectively communicating the long-term value and risk mitigation aspects of cyber security.

- **Complexity and intangibility:** Cyber security outcomes often involve intangible elements, such as enhanced resilience against cyber threats or improved data security, and the value of these might not be immediately quantifiable in traditional terms.

- **Difficulty in quantification:** While some cyber security benefits can be quantified, such as potential cost savings from avoiding a data breach, others are challenging to express in monetary terms. The prevention of reputational damage, protection of intellectual property or the assurance of regulatory compliance may contribute significant value but are intricate to measure precisely.

- **Value fluidity:** The dynamic nature of the cyber security landscape, coupled with evolving organisational needs and external factors, may influence the perceived value. Several factors can contribute to this fluidity, such as emerging threat landscape, technological advancements, shifts in the regulatory landscape, transformations in the IT infrastructure, etc.

Continual monitoring, risk assessments and periodic reviews of the cyber security strategy are crucial to ensuring that the identified value remains aligned with the organisation's evolving needs and the ever-changing cyber security landscape. Regular updates to the business case may be necessary to reflect these changes and maintain the relevance and effectiveness of cyber security measures.

The cyber security business case: an arduous challenge

Daniel Desruisseaux's two-part blog, 'The Cyber Security Business Case: An Arduous Challenge' (2017), states that a typical cyber security business case comprises three key elements for financial analysis. First, an estimate of the revenue or cost savings a proposed project may generate. Second, the costs to implement the project. Third, a formula to calculate the net financial value of the project for comparison across potential investments. This allows companies to allocate a portion of their limited funds to the proposals projected to serve the company's interests best. Although specific to a domain, it provides an insight into the details.

Creating such a business case for cyber security investments is uniquely challenging. Determining the costs requires creating a comprehensive security plan that audits the current infrastructure, policies and training to identify needed upgrades to reach target security levels. This complex plan has an expensive price tag and details the required capital expenditures for security devices, architecture changes, etc.

Estimating the financial benefits of a cyber security project proves even more difficult. Quantifying the likelihood and cost impact of prevented cyber attacks targeting industrial control systems is arduous, given the lack of publicly available data. The network breaches could lead to downtime, intellectual property theft, ransom demands or reputation loss – all costly and complex to reliably calculate.

Experts recommend gathering better financial data by funding a thorough security plan focused first on higher risks. Consult peers, vendors and industry events to estimate attack likelihood and potential impact costs for vulnerabilities highlighted in the plan. However, most cyber security projects still gain approvals even with imprecise financial projections because companies recognise the existential downside risks outweigh the uncertainty. They see more value in risk mitigation than in an elusive detailed cost–benefit analysis (Desruisseaux, 2017).

THE ART OF NEGOTIATION

The art of negotiation is a complex and dynamic skill that involves the ability to reach mutually beneficial agreements through communication, persuasion and adapting accordingly. It is a multifaceted skill involving effective communication, active listening and a keen understanding of one's interests and those of the other parties involved.

Building positive relationships, understanding underlying interests and demonstrating emotional intelligence are crucial. Problem-solving skills, patience and perseverance contribute to navigating challenges while maintaining a win–win mindset and fostering collaboration and ethical considerations to uphold integrity.

Mastering this skill is an ongoing process that combines interpersonal skills, strategic thinking and adaptability to create positive outcomes in various scenarios, and that requires reflection, adaptation and a commitment to improvement.

Business analysts, often acting as mediators between various stakeholders, need to employ negotiation skills to reconcile conflicting interests and drive consensus. The ability to understand the underlying needs and concerns of different parties, coupled with active listening and effective communication, enables business analysts to craft solutions that satisfy diverse requirements. Negotiation becomes even more crucial when dealing with cyber security business cases. In this context, the negotiation process goes beyond aligning business goals and involves convincing decision-makers about the imperative nature of cyber security investments.

Furthermore, the art of negotiation extends to communicating the value proposition of cyber security initiatives in terms that resonate with diverse stakeholders. Whether emphasising regulatory compliance, safeguarding customer trust or protecting brand reputation, effective negotiation skills are indispensable for gaining support and resources for cyber security endeavours.

REFLECTION TIME

Take a moment, ponder and write down:

- Evaluate your current methods for aligning cyber security initiatives with broader business objectives. How can you strengthen this alignment to position security measures as strategic enablers rather than isolated necessities?

The negotiator

My younger son was a handful when he was a little boy. Emulating his elder brother all the time, he preferred watching TV programmes for five-year-olds instead of baby programmes such as *Teletubbies*. He never wanted me to hold his hand when walking, convinced that being a big boy like his brother meant he could manage independently. To address this, I explained that I needed his help navigating crowded streets so we wouldn't accidentally bump into people. That worked like magic, and from that day, whenever we stepped out, he would look out for his mum like a capable big boy.

Growing up, he consistently used negotiation to get his way. Determined and persistent, he would engage in discussions to persuade and negotiate. As a mother, I had to adapt, seeking alternative and creative strategies to handle various situations. Regardless, one constant was our commitment to discussing and understanding each other's concerns and engaging in negotiation to arrive at mutually agreeable solutions. Even now, as a teenager, this approach is continued, as the toys are different, but the need remains.

Drawing parallels from this personal anecdote, the toddler's understanding of the need to secure something, exemplified by his protective stance towards his mum, mirrors the importance of negotiation skills in reference to cyber security business cases. These skills are pivotal in articulating perspectives effectively to decision-makers. It involves comprehending their viewpoints, presenting details in a language accessible to them and accentuating the tangible benefits encapsulated in the critical question 'What's in it for them?' This analogy demonstrates how negotiation is not just a communication tool but a strategic approach to convey the significance of cyber security investments in a language that resonates with decision-makers, ultimately ensuring mutual understanding and support.

CYBER SECURITY POLICY

Transitioning from the business case, this section focuses on formulating cyber security policies – the guiding principles that shape an organisation's approach to security.

Creating and writing a cyber security policy typically involves collaboration among various stakeholders within an organisation. The responsibility may fall under the purview of the chief information security officer (CISO) or a dedicated cyber security team. However, the process often requires input from IT professionals, legal experts, compliance officers and other relevant departments.

The cyber security policy outlines guidelines and measures to safeguard an organisation's information systems and data from potential threats, ensuring information confidentiality, integrity and availability. The policy must align with industry regulations, legal requirements and the specific needs of the organisation. Therefore, a cross-functional team with expertise in cyber security, legal compliance and IT governance is usually involved in drafting and maintaining the cyber security policy.

COMPONENTS OF A CYBER SECURITY POLICY

A comprehensive cyber security policy typically consists of aspects from Figure 2.3, 'Overview of cyber security knowledge for business analysts', in Chapter 2. While the specific elements may vary based on the organisation's size, industry and regulatory requirements, the following are standard components found in many cyber security policies:

- Introduction and purpose:
  - Overview of the policy's purpose and importance.
  - Explanation of the organisation's commitment to cyber security.
- Scope:
  - Clearly defines the scope of the policy, specifying which systems, data and personnel are covered.
- Policy governance:
  - Identification of responsible parties, such as the CISO or relevant security team.
  - Roles and responsibilities of key stakeholders in implementing and enforcing the policy.
- Information classification and handling:
  - Guidelines for classifying information based on sensitivity.
  - Procedures for handling, storing and transmitting different classifications of information.
- Access controls:
  - User authentication and authorisation procedures.
  - Principle of least privilege to limit access based on job roles.
- Data encryption:
  - Policies related to encrypting data in transit and at rest to protect confidentiality.
- Incident response and reporting:
  - Procedures for reporting security incidents.
  - Steps to be taken during and after a security incident, including communication protocols.
- Security awareness and training:
  - Requirements for ongoing cyber security training and awareness programmes for employees.
- Physical security:
  - Guidelines for securing physical access to facilities and equipment housing sensitive information.
- Network security:
  - Best practices for securing network infrastructure.
- Endpoint security:
  - Policies related to securing end-user devices, such as laptops, desktops and mobile devices.
- Patch management:
  - Procedures for keeping software, operating systems and applications up-to-date with the latest security patches.

- Vulnerability management:
  - Guidelines for identifying, assessing and mitigating vulnerabilities in systems and software.
- Third-party security:
  - Security requirements for third-party vendors and partners with access to the organisation's systems or data.
- Compliance and legal requirements:
  - Ensures the policy aligns with relevant industry regulations, standards and legal requirements.
- Audit and monitoring:
  - Policies related to ongoing monitoring of security controls and regular audits to ensure compliance.
- Employee responsibilities and code of conduct:
  - Expectations of employees regarding their role in maintaining cyber security.
  - Code of conduct related to information security.
- Remote work and BYOD:
  - Guidelines for securing remote work environments and personal devices used for work.
- Business continuity and disaster recovery:
  - Procedures for ensuring business continuity and recovering from cyber security incidents.
- Documented exceptions and waivers:
  - Process for documenting and justifying exceptions to security policies

The key components ensure that the policy is not just regulatory checkboxes but a living document that fosters a culture of security resilience.

Business analyst support

Business analysts can play a crucial role in supporting the development, implementation and adherence to cyber security policies within an organisation.

They can be instrumental in translating technical security requirements into solutions that align with the broader business objectives. They serve as a crucial link between the technical intricacies of cyber security and the overarching goals of the organisation. Business analysts can ensure that the cyber security policy addresses threats and is tailored to meet the specific needs and strategic direction of the business.

One of the key strengths of business analysts lies in their proficiency in eliciting and documenting requirements. In the context of cyber security policies, business analysts can collaborate closely with stakeholders to identify and articulate specific security needs to help create a foundation for policies that are effective in enhancing security posture and well-aligned with the organisational context.

Active participation in risk assessments is another vital role that business analysts can play in the cyber security domain. By collaborating with security experts, business analysts can contribute to identifying and evaluating potential risks and threats. This involvement ensures that cyber security policies are grounded in a thorough understanding of the risks faced by the organisation, allowing for a more targeted and effective security strategy.

Effective communication is a hallmark of business analysts, and this skill is particularly valuable when bridging the communication gap between technical security teams and business stakeholders. Business analysts facilitate meaningful discussions, ensuring that the importance of cyber security policies is communicated clearly. By engaging stakeholders in the cyber security dialogue, business analysts contribute to a collective understanding of the security landscape and foster a culture of security awareness.

Clarity and comprehensiveness of policy documentation are critical for the successful implementation of cyber security measures. Business analysts can leverage their documentation skills to create policies that are accessible and understandable to both technical and non-technical stakeholders. Well-documented policies enhance transparency, making it easier for all stakeholders to comprehend and adhere to security guidelines.

From understanding business needs to active involvement in risk assessments and effective communication, business analysts can contribute to fortifying an organisation's security posture through a solid cyber security policy.

REFLECTION TIME

Take a moment, ponder and write down:

- Reflect on your current understanding of cyber security policy and the implications for your organisation. What steps would you like to take to better support policy development and implementation?

SUMMARY

This chapter focused on the two components, cyber security business case and cyber security policy, within the broader framework, which are capable of standing alone or seamlessly integrating with the overall structure.

They reinforce the symbiotic relationship between strategic planning and operational implementation. The cyber security business case sets the stage for understanding why cyber security investments are crucial while aligning with organisational objectives, and the cyber security policy provides the necessary guidelines to implement these strategies effectively.

This dual nature allows you to choose your entry point, making the framework adaptable to your learning needs. Whether you are focused on strategic decision-making or the tactical implementation of cyber security measures, this chapter and the integrated framework offer a comprehensive and flexible resource for understanding and navigating the complex landscape of cyber security management.

TAKEAWAY QUESTIONS

- What are your key learning points in this chapter?
- What is the one lesson that you'll implement?
- How do you aim to contribute towards keeping the cyber security policy active and to include cyber elements in the business cases?

10 THE INNER COMPASS

Here's what you'll learn from this chapter:

- Bringing it all together.
- What ethics are.
- Ethical ignorance and concerns.
- The IIBA Code of Ethical Conduct.
- Ethics in cyber security.
- Sustaining the inner compass.

This final chapter delves into the critical aspect of ethics within the Business Analysis and Cyber Security Framework. Just as mindset serves as the foundation, ethics are equally essential. Without ethical considerations, the entire framework will be ineffective. Before delving into this crucial aspect, here is a recap of the whole framework.

CHAPTER 1 SUMMARY

Chapter 1 explored the fundamentals of business analysis and the pivotal role of a business analyst. The exploration began with a clear understanding of business analysis and a nuanced exploration of the business analyst's identity, followed by the practical aspects of analysis in action, understanding solution options and the far-reaching impacts of incomplete analysis through real-world scenarios.

The chapter emphasised the weight of responsibility that comes with the role of a business analyst, underlining the significance of clarity in role and responsibility definitions. It challenged you to reflect on the profound meaning the profession holds, and encouraged a thoughtful examination of perspectives on various business analysis activities.

Finally, it focused on the importance of clarity in understanding the responsibilities of one's role, drawing parallels with the anecdote of the third bricklayer. It encouraged self-reflection, questioning whether you are in the role intentionally or by happenstance, emphasising the need to dedicate your full attention to the responsibilities of the position. It highlighted the undocumented trust between a business analyst and a client, which is built by consistently delivering thorough analysis and positioning yourself as a trusted advisor who provides stakeholders with the necessary facts and perspectives for informed decision-making.

The chapter concluded with a thought-provoking question: as a trusted advisor, can a business analyst exclude cyber security from their analysis, by assuming that technical teams handle all cyber security-related requirements? Asserting that non-functional requirements alone do not encompass all cyber security requirements, this chapter set the stage for further exploration.

CHAPTER 2 SUMMARY

Chapter 2 explored the varied perceptions of cyber security and its significance in different professional roles. The narrative transitioned to a personal experience involving a low-priority enhancement project, revealing the critical risk overlooked by the organisation. This incident catalysed the journey into cyber security.

The chapter then delved into real-world incidents, such as those involving HMRC and TalkTalk, to spotlight the consequences of cyber security lapses, taking a step back to consider the evolving technological landscape and the potential vulnerabilities arising from global interconnected systems.

Exploring the analogy of finite and infinite games, inspired by Simon Sinek's insights, the chapter highlighted the clash between short-term gains and long-term sustainability. The narrative expanded to address the role of business analysts in the cyber security domain, while acknowledging that business analysts need not be cyber security experts. The chapter emphasised the importance of integrating security into project inception and holistically expanding the analyst's scope to include cyber security. The necessity for foundational cyber security knowledge among business analysts was underscored, setting the stage for further exploration in subsequent chapters.

CHAPTER 3 SUMMARY

Chapter 3 introduced the Business Analysis and Cyber Security Framework, designed to empower business analysts in incorporating cyber security aspects throughout project development phases. The chapter explored key concepts within the Business Analysis and Cyber Security Framework, beginning with the elucidation of the term 'cyber', commonly associated with the internet, digital or the virtual world. Security, defined as 'the state of being free from danger or threat', was presented as protection for a valued possession against potential threats.

As the framework's first building block, the 'security mindset' aimed to equip business analysts with the awareness and approach necessary to navigate the ever-changing landscape of social trends and business needs. Recognising the inevitability of technological and procedural changes, the chapter stressed the importance of assessing unintended impacts alongside intended ones when proposing solution options.

The security mindset, presented as a valuable tool in a business analyst's arsenal, was highlighted for its role in discovering unintended impacts and ensuring a holistic approach to addressing evolving business requirements.

CHAPTER 4 SUMMARY

Chapter 4 delved into one of the two key pillars, 'risk analysis' within the Business Analysis and Cyber Security Framework. The exploration commenced by unravelling the significance of risk within the context of cyber security and unfolded with an in-depth exploration of risk management processes, shedding light on the integral role of business analysts in this domain.

The narrative extended into a thought-provoking story about a mousetrap from Manoj Vasudevan. Through this narrative, the chapter emphasised the universal responsibility for security and the necessity for leaders to anticipate and prepare for risks rather than react in panic.

A key takeaway highlighted the human tendency to ignore apparent risks, underscoring the importance of identifying and managing risks for effective security. Douglas Adams's quote encapsulated the essence, emphasising that security is about managing risks and true security is achieved when all risks are identified and managed.

The chapter proceeded to define risk and present an overview of the ISO 31000 risk management process. Business analysts' roles at various stages of the process were elucidated, emphasising their contribution to analysing impacts, facilitating communication and ensuring cyber resilience.

Predictable surprises and existential risks were discussed in the context of acknowledging the unprecedented changes in social, economic and environmental landscapes. The chapter advocated a 'premortem exercise' to identify and prepare for 'predictable surprises'. Business analysts were positioned as instrumental in supporting the identification of these surprises and influencing strategic decisions.

The chapter also addressed bias in risk perception, acknowledging the impact of cognitive biases on decision-making. Barriers to effective risk management were highlighted, emphasising the need for cultural changes and improved communication. A glimpse into harnessing AI concluded the chapter, suggesting its potential to enhance risk management with advanced analytics, automation and predictive capabilities.

CHAPTER 5 SUMMARY

This chapter emphasised the role of common sense in business analysis, drawing parallels to James Madison's notion that 'Philosophy is common sense with big words'. Business analysis was portrayed as common sense with structure, highlighting its crucial position in various professions.

Business analysts were depicted as leveraging different models and frameworks, each contributing unique strengths and weaknesses. Despite their diversity, these models converged at the compilation of requirements essential for addressing identified business needs. The structured and comprehensive approach provided by these models guide analysts through systematic explorations of the business environment.

A story about 'The Three Little Pigs' illustrated three key lessons: understanding the objective's intention, recognising the nature of threats and acknowledging the knowledge and effort required to build a suitable solution.

The chapter delved into IIBA's Business Analysis Knowledge Areas, listing knowledge areas and noting cyber security touchpoints. It reiterated that business analysts should call upon cyber security SMEs when needed.

The chapter concluded with a checklist for the cyber security extended BACCM.

CHAPTER 6 SUMMARY

This chapter aimed to address the concept of 'shift left' by providing pointers to incorporate relevant cyber security discussions at every stage of the project. It emphasised that, due to organisational and project differences, there is no one-size-fits-all approach to cyber security, and the provided pointers should be considered as guidelines to trigger the security mindset and involve security expertise throughout the project life cycle.

The metaphor 'when you pick up one end of the stick, you also pick up the other' highlighted that actions or decisions often come with positive and negative consequences or responsibilities. The story about the old boilermaker illustrated the importance of experience and practical wisdom in quickly identifying issues, reflecting the role of a skilled analyst in business analysis.

The chapter accentuated the significance of using the right tools for the right job in business analysis. It underlined that the art of business analysis lies in understanding the diverse toolbox and judiciously selecting the most fitting tool for addressing specific problems.

The extension of cyber security into different knowledge areas and activities highlights that collaboration between business analysts and cyber security stakeholders is crucial to creating more secure and resilient systems.

To summarise, the chapter focused on the concept of 'shifting left' in cyber security, advocating for the strategic integration of security considerations throughout the project life cycle. It provided practical pointers for business analysts to bring cyber security discussions to the table at the right time, ensuring that cyber security is an integral part of the project from the beginning rather than an afterthought. The chapter aimed to set the stage for a proactive and holistic approach to security, recognising the unique context of each organisation and project.

CHAPTER 7 SUMMARY

In this chapter the focus shifted to the domain of data security, emphasising the need to safeguard the 'crown jewels' of an organisation. The chapter began by likening data to the lifeblood of modern society, drawing parallels with the circulatory system and emphasising the importance of responsible management to prevent contamination or infection.

The exponential growth of global data volume, projected to reach 175 zettabytes by 2025, was highlighted, accentuating the challenge of managing an overwhelming amount of data. The distinction between data security and cyber security was clarified, leading to a discussion on the various states of data throughout their life cycle.

The approach to data security mirrored that of cyber security, focusing on identifying risks with a security mindset. Business analysts were positioned as key contributors to data security activities, particularly in securing process flows against cyber threats and ensuring compliance.

The chapter concluded by exploring emerging data trends, illuminating data as the new currency, introducing a data risk framework and discussing potential pitfalls in managing Big Data. Overall, the chapter provided insights into the dynamic landscape of data security, offering perspectives on contemporary challenges and opportunities in managing and securing data.

CHAPTER 8 SUMMARY

This chapter focused on people management, personas, misuse cases, incident management and business continuity planning in the context of cyber security.

The chapter began by emphasising that people are often the weakest link in cyber security, and managing them is crucial to preventing security breaches, as human errors contribute significantly to such incidents. The vulnerability of human factors in cyber security was discussed, highlighting the role of human errors, intentional or unintentional, in contributing to security breaches.

The concept of developing personas and detailed character profiles representing different user types was introduced. These personas aid in human-centred design, ensuring cyber security strategies align with diverse user needs. Various cyber security personas were presented, including those unintentionally posing risks and those with malicious intent.

Business analysts were encouraged to develop misuse cases alongside use cases to understand how threat actors could intentionally compromise or misuse the system. Collaboration with business, security and IT teams was emphasised to effectively identify and mitigate threat scenarios.

An analogy involving the growth of bamboo illustrated the importance of incident management. The story highlighted the need for proactive planning and readiness, emphasising that incidents cannot be entirely avoided but can be managed effectively.

The chapter also explored BCP, with business analysts playing a supportive role. Their communication, analysis and documentation skills were deemed valuable in contributing to the various phases of BCP, including business impact analysis, risk assessment, recovery strategies, training and maintenance/review.

A narrative about a farmer on a windy sea coast underscored the importance of preparedness, proactive planning and a well-defined incident management and business continuity strategy. The story demonstrated that incidents are inevitable, just like the winds, and organisations should focus on learning from incidents and improving their cyber security posture to emerge stronger.

CHAPTER 9 SUMMARY

Chapter 9 focused on the cyber security business case and cyber security policy within the broader Business Analysis and Cyber Security Framework, serving as guardians of cyber resilience for organisations.

The chapter began by describing the importance of a 'good' business case that effectively answers the question 'What's in it for the decision-maker?'

The cyber security business case was highlighted as a strategic blueprint for cyber security investments. Business analyst support in crafting a compelling business case was discussed, along with the six foundational principles proposed by Christian Hyatt for engaging executive decision-makers and insights from Daniel Desruisseaux's blog on the challenges of creating a cyber security business case, defining the three critical elements for financial analysis.

The chapter drew parallels between negotiation skills and a toddler's protective stance, showcasing the importance of effective negotiation when presenting cyber security business cases to decision-makers. Negotiation was portrayed not just as a communication tool but a complex skill involving effective communication, active listening, understanding the interests of all parties involved and a strategic approach to conveying the significance of cyber security investments.

Transitioning from the business case, the chapter focused on formulating cyber security policies. These policies were described as guiding principles shaping an organisation's approach to security. Standard components found in many cyber security policies were outlined, and the role of business analysts in supporting the development, implementation and adherence to these policies was summarised.

The chapter concluded by reinforcing the dual nature of the cyber security business case and policy, which are capable of standing alone or seamlessly integrating into the overall framework. It highlighted the symbiotic relationship between strategic planning and operational implementation, offering you flexibility in choosing your entry point based on strategic decision-making or tactical implementation needs.

BRINGING IT ALL TOGETHER

The elements of this framework are versatile, allowing for their adaptable deployment, whether as individual components tailored to an organisation's and project's unique requirements or collectively to construct secure and resilient systems. Incorporating cyber security components not only furnishes a foundational backdrop but also provides guidance on how business analysts can effectively contribute to each element.

Figure 10.1 Business Analysis and Cyber Security Framework with ethics (Copyright: I-Perceptions Consulting Ltd)

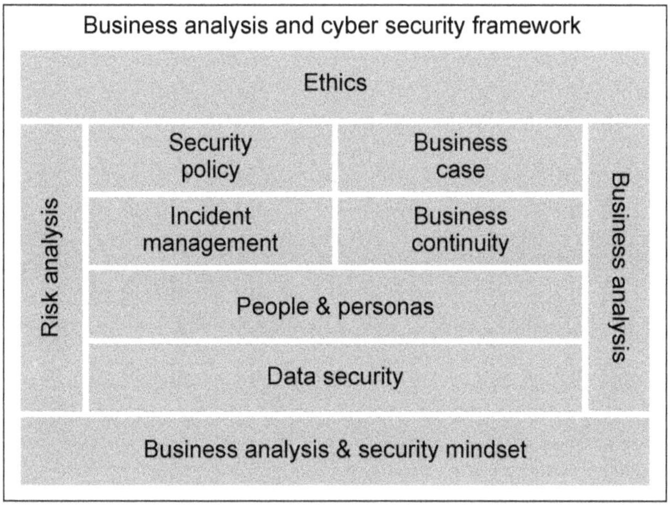

Like the foundational mindset, ethics serve as the cornerstone in shaping the application and integration of these components, without which no other facets of the framework can effectively operate or be precisely executed (Figure 10.1). Ethics intertwine with each facet like an invisible thread, directing not just the technicalities but also fostering the framework that upholds principles and values, paving the way for conscientious and responsible practices within business analysis and cyber security.

WHAT ARE ETHICS?

Ethics refer to the branch of philosophy that deals with the principles of morality and the concept of right and wrong. It involves the study and application of values, principles and guidelines that govern human behaviour in various contexts.[5]

Ethical considerations guide individuals and groups in making decisions and taking actions that are morally sound, fair and socially responsible. Ethical standards provide a framework for responsible conduct and ensure that choices align with accepted principles of fairness, integrity and respect for others. Ethical behaviour involves a conscious effort to consider the impact of one's actions on individuals and society as a whole.

Ethical ignorance is not a bliss

In a world increasingly shaped by complex moral dilemmas and intricate decision-making, the significance of ethical awareness cannot be overstated. Ethical ignorance cannot be a bliss, turning a blind eye to ethical considerations is not a pathway to take.

---

5   https://www.dictionary.com/browse/ethics

Instead, it emphasises the imperative of acknowledging, understanding and actively addressing ethical dimensions.

As mentioned in Chapter 3, the Facebook 'Like' button was initially intended to share positivity. However, the social impacts span much more broadly, and researchers are uncovering the psychological effects that social media interactions can have on well-being.

Jan Fox, in his article 'An unlikeable truth' (Fox, 2018), raises concerns about psychological manipulation and emotional exploitation. The deliberate design to make these features addictive, likened to 'behavioural cocaine', raises ethical questions about the responsibility of social media platforms in shaping user behaviours for their benefit. The potential for addiction, stress-inducing behaviours and the impact on mental health, especially among younger generations, highlights ethical considerations related to user well-being and the duty of platforms to prioritise user welfare over engagement metrics.

The ease with which these buttons facilitate emotional expression may contribute to a culture where users prioritise quick, emotional reactions over thoughtful engagement. Ethical concerns arise as these platforms influence attitudes, perceptions and societal norms, potentially contributing to the spread of misinformation.

Furthermore, the psychological impact of seeking social validation through likes and reactions prompts ethical discussions about the platform's role in manipulating users' emotional states for prolonged engagement. Emphasising emotional responses over reasoned discourse may lead to ethical lapses in critical thinking, accountability and responsible information-sharing.

Ethical concerns

Both Albert Einstein and J. Robert Oppenheimer, key figures in the development of the atomic bomb during the Second World War, expressed regret and ethical concerns regarding their involvement in the project. Einstein, while not directly part of the Manhattan Project, regretted signing a letter urging President Roosevelt to pursue atomic research and later expressed remorse for the bombings of Hiroshima and Nagasaki (Philipson, 2024). Oppenheimer, the project's scientific director, grappled with the ethical implications of creating a weapon with devastating consequences, and, after witnessing the destructive power of the bomb, famously quoted the Bhagavad Gita, 'Now, I become Death, the destroyer of worlds', conveying the weight of his ethical dilemma (Nolan, 2023).

Their regret underscores the deep ethical considerations associated with scientific advancements, especially those with destructive potential. The complex feelings of both Einstein and Oppenheimer emphasise that ethical considerations cannot be ignored or compromised in the pursuit of scientific progress. Their experiences serve as a cautionary tale, highlighting the lasting moral responsibility that accompanies decisions with far-reaching consequences. The ethical dimensions of scientific endeavours must be carefully weighed and acknowledged to prevent unforeseen harm and ensure the responsible use of knowledge and technology.

CODE OF CONDUCT

The BCS Code of Conduct[6] serves as a foundational document outlining the ethical principles and professional standards expected of members within BCS, The Chartered Insititute for IT (The British Computer Society). It is designed to ensure that professionals in the field of computing uphold the highest standards of integrity, competence and accountability in their work.

By adhering to the four fundamental principles, 'Professional Integrity', 'Competence and Professional Development', ' Duty to the Public Interest' and 'Professional Responsibility', members of BCS uphold the highest standards in their professional practice, thereby promoting trust, integrity and professionalism within the computing profession (BCS, 2024).

The IIBA Code of Ethical Conduct and Professional Standards[7] is a mandatory set of guidelines applicable to pursuing or holding certifications in business analysis and responsibilities to the profession, client and the public. It seeks to establish a foundation for ethical business analysis practices, emphasising integrity, professionalism and responsible conduct across various dimensions of the profession.

ETHICS IN CYBER SECURITY

In *The Ethics of Cybersecurity* (Loi and Christen, 2020), Michele Loi and Markus Christen provide a comprehensive examination of various ethical frameworks applicable to cyber security. It begins with an exploration of two principal frameworks: **the principlist approach**, which is significant in cyber security research and outlined in the *Menlo Report* (Dittrich and Kenneally, 2011), and **the rights-based principle**, especially pertinent within EU law. Both frameworks grapple with the inherent probabilistic nature of harms and benefits associated with cyber security, necessitating considering risk and probability.

Loi and Christen delve into the ethics of risk, discussing consequentialist approaches, which is an ethical theory that judges the morality of actions based on their outcomes or consequences rather than the intrinsic nature of the actions themselves.

Utilitarianism is a consequentialist ethical theory that evaluates the moral worth of actions based on the principle of maximising overall happiness or well-being. By applying utilitarian principles in the design and development of electric vehicles, manufacturers aim to create products that provide the greatest overall benefit to society, considering factors such as environmental impact, affordability, safety and convenience.

The development of antivirus software is another example that demonstrates utilitarianism in product development by prioritising the maximisation of overall utility or benefit for society through the protection of users, minimisation of harm and promotion of trust in combating cybercrime.

---

6   https://www.bcs.org/membership-and-registrations/become-a-member/bcs-code-of-conduct/

7   https://www.iiba.org/globalassets/documents/terms-conditions-codes-of-conduct/certification-code-of-ethical-conduct-and-professional-standards.pdf

Maximin consequentialism is a variation of consequentialist ethical theory focusing on minimising the worst possible outcome or maximising the well-being of the least advantaged. By applying maximin consequentialism, automobile manufacturers prioritise the development and implementation of safety features such as airbags, seat belts and crumple zones that provide the greatest protection in worst-case scenarios. Even if these safety features may not enhance the overall driving experience or performance of the vehicle, they are considered essential for minimising the maximum possible harm in the event of an accident.

Another example is the end-to-end encryption that ensures messages sent between users are encrypted on the sender's device and can only be decrypted by the intended recipient, thereby protecting the confidentiality and integrity of the communication. While implementing end-to-end encryption may introduce additional complexity and computational overhead, it significantly reduces the risk of unauthorised interception or surveillance of sensitive communications, particularly in high-risk environments such as those involving political dissidents or journalists.

Deontological ethics is the theory focusing on the inherent nature of actions rather than the consequences they produce. It provides a framework for evaluating the morality of actions based on principles of duty, rights and justice, rather than solely on their outcomes. Deontological ethical theory could be applied in adherence to strict safety standards in the manufacturing of children's toys by investing in high-quality materials, rigorous testing procedures and safety certifications to ensure that their toys meet or exceed regulatory safety standards.

By incorporating end-to-end encryption into messaging applications, organisations uphold deontological principles such as respecting users' autonomy, protecting their confidential communications and safeguarding their privacy rights, even in the face of potential challenges such as limitations on data analysis or surveillance.

Loi and Christen also examine the 'contextual integrity' approach of Helen Nissenbaum, a framework for understanding privacy in the digital age. They then recommend a general methodology for the ethical assessment of cyber security technology by extending Nissenbaum's framework to encompass a broader range of social norms and expectations related to human interactions within a practice affected by cyber security.

This extended framework includes steps to evaluate prevailing contexts, information attributes, changes in societal norms brought by cyber security measures and their alignment with socially valuable goals and core values and rights.

Relevance to business analysis

Business analysts often deal with sensitive information and collaborate with various stakeholders. Upholding ethical standards involves ensuring transparency in communication, respecting confidentiality and building trust with stakeholders. This is crucial for maintaining positive relationships and fostering a trustworthy business environment. With the increasing reliance on data, business analysts must adhere to regulations, respect individual privacy rights and implement measures to safeguard sensitive information during the analysis process.

Ethical business analysis emphasises the importance of providing accurate and complete information to stakeholders. Business analysts must ensure that decision-makers have the necessary data and insights to make informed choices. This aligns with ethical principles such as integrity and honesty. It also involves navigating potential conflicts of interest and ensuring fairness in decision-making. Business analysts should approach their work with impartiality, avoiding bias and considering the impact of recommendations on all stakeholders equitably.

In the era of digital transformation, business analysts often work with advanced technologies. Ethical business analysis involves ensuring the responsible and ethical use of technology, considering the potential social, economic and environmental impacts of technological solutions.

Ethical business analysis extends beyond immediate stakeholders to consider broader societal and environmental impacts. Business analysts should be mindful of the moral implications of business decisions on communities, the environment and society.

Tech ethics

Raina Kumra, in her 'Tech Ethics: Avoiding Unintended Consequences' training (Kumra, 2020), introduces the 'Wheel of Misfortune', identifying eight emerging risks crucial for understanding and addressing ethical concerns in technology. Acknowledging the personal responsibility of creators and consumers, she urges envisioning future scenarios and assessing potential risks. These risk categories, developed in collaboration with the Institute for the Future, encompass truth, addiction, economic disparities, algorithmic biases, surveillance, data control, trust and criminal actors.

Kumra proposes a comprehensive checklist to build ethical products considering present and future vulnerabilities. Sample questions include addressing bias in training data, ensuring understandable terms of service, preparing for data breaches and mitigating the spread of misinformation. Customising the checklist involves collaborative efforts within the team, identifying relevant questions and incorporating them into product design requirements. Accountability is emphasised by assigning individuals to run and review the checklist, ensuring a continuous ethical approach, even in minor feature updates.

In the unregulated tech industry, where self-regulation is pivotal, every team member's commitment to ethics becomes crucial. Raina Kumra highlights the need for ongoing vigilance and ethical considerations across the organisation, underlining the role of self-regulation until formal regulations are established.

Through a business analysis lens

Kumra's proposed checklist becomes a practical guide for business analysts, offering questions to assess the ethical implications of their work. This checklist includes considerations for data bias, user comprehension, data breach preparedness and content integrity. Collaborative customisation allows teams to adapt the checklist to their specific projects, reinforcing accountability and ethical implementation.

The framework's call for self-regulation resonates with business analysts, emphasising the need to uphold ethical standards in the absence of industry-wide regulations. This highlights the significance of incorporating ethical considerations in significant product launches and minor feature updates and enhancements.

In conclusion, business analysts can be positioned as ethical gatekeepers in the tech industry, leveraging frameworks and checklists to embed ethical principles into their practices. This proactive approach aligns with industry best practices and prepares the tech sector for a future where moral considerations are paramount.

Through a cyber security lens

The risk categories, ranging from truth and addiction to surveillance and criminal actors, align with the multifaceted challenges faced in cyber security.

Addressing biases in training data, ensuring transparent terms of service and preparing for data breaches are ethical imperatives and integral components of a robust cyber security strategy. The emphasis on accountability resonates strongly in the cyber security domain, where the consequences of lapses can be severe.

Moreover, the collaborative nature of customising the checklist aligns with the interdisciplinary approach often required in cyber security efforts. Incorporating ethical considerations into product design, a theme highlighted by Kumra, is crucial to developing secure and responsible technological solutions.

Security must go hand in hand with privacy and ethical use of data. It emphasises protecting data from external threats, ensuring security practices align with ethical considerations and respecting user privacy. This entails striking a balance between robust security measures and the responsible use of data, acknowledging that unchecked surveillance or data collection can infringe on individuals' rights.

Self-regulation and a commitment to ethics are foundational in cyber security practices in an unregulated tech landscape. The constant vigilance and proactive stance recommended by Kumra mirror the cyber security principle of staying ahead of evolving threats. Ethical considerations in data control, trust and privacy are central to maintaining the integrity and resilience of cyber security measures.

SUSTAINING THE INNER COMPASS

Being ethical is not just a moral imperative but an intrinsic characteristic embedded in the essence of being human. This inherent ethical dimension shapes human interactions, decisions and the pursuit of a harmonious existence. The intricate interplay of cognition, emotions and social dynamics contributes to the development of an internal value system that serves as a guiding force for individuals.

At the cognitive level, humans possess the ability to reason, discern right from wrong and make moral judgements. This intellectual prowess forms the foundation of an internal ethical compass, guiding individuals through the complex terrain of ethical considerations. The capacity to reflect on the consequences of actions and align choices with moral principles is a distinctive feature of the human psyche.

For business analysts, leveraging this internal value system can be a transformative and guiding force in their professional endeavours. The ethical compass within each analyst can serve as a reference point for making decisions that align with moral principles and societal expectations. Ethical considerations become an integral part of the analysis process, influencing choices related to data handling, and how stakeholders are engaged, dealing with privacy issues, data protection and digital integrity, and creating decision-making protocols that demand heightened ethical awareness. Understanding the moral implications of actions and decisions is a professional responsibility and an expression of your inherent humanity.

An ethically informed internal value system guides analysts to navigate complex scenarios with integrity and transparency. It promotes responsible practices in analysis, ensuring that ethical considerations are not compromised for short-term gains. This internal ethical compass becomes a beacon, illuminating the path towards sustainable and socially responsible business practices.

In conclusion, successfully implementing the Business Analysis and Cyber Security Framework is not just a technical achievement, but a testament to the organisation's commitment to resilience, ethical conduct and future readiness. By intertwining these critical components, we create a robust shield that protects against the evolving landscape of cyber threats and fosters a culture of security, innovation and sustained success. The synergy of business analysis and cyber security, underpinned by the surrounding structure of mindset, ethics, risk and business analysis, propels the organisation towards a secure and ethical future.

Storytime

A final narrative, which gradually unfolded its depth over time, has made itself my enduring favourite, a timeless legend that I heard many years back. The tale possesses a unique ability to anchor me to the present moment, serves as a powerful reminder to perceive reality as it is and encourages me to explore situations from diverse perspectives. The resonance of this story continues to be a source of grounding and introspection, shaping my outlook on life with its profound wisdom. The narrative has been slightly adjusted to align with the context being discussed in this book.

A wise monk resided in quiet contemplation in a secluded corner of the world, nestled amid serene landscapes. His days were spent in communion with nature, and he had a devoted disciple eager to absorb the wisdom that emanated from the monk's tranquil existence.

One day, the monk, sensing the need for solitude, announced to his disciple that he would temporarily leave their sanctuary. He entrusted the disciple with the responsibility of looking after their sacred abode in his absence. Intrigued and earnest, the disciple, inquisitive about the nature of his duty, approached the monk with a sincere question: 'How can I fulfil this task entrusted to me?'

With a serene gaze and a gentle smile, the monk uttered a single word – 'awareness'. Perplexed but respectful, the disciple accepted this cryptic guidance and commenced his stewardship with a commitment to understand the depth behind the monk's enigmatic counsel.

As days passed, the disciple still grappled with the true essence of his master's advice. Seeking clarity, he returned to the monk and sought further enlightenment. Once again, the monk, with unwavering calmness, repeated the same word – 'awareness'.

Undeterred by the apparent simplicity of the response, the disciple returned again, his heart earnest and his mind seeking comprehension. Like a steady beacon of wisdom, the monk uttered the familiar word – 'awareness'.

The disciple earnestly embraced his duties in his master's absence, diligently maintaining the sanctuary. He ensured the hut was clean and ventured to the farmers' market weekly to procure essentials such as firewood, vegetables and grains. As the rains reduced the supply of firewood, he adjusted his budget to allocate more funds, prioritising warmth and safety.

One week, the market offered no firewood, leaving him cold and anxious about potential animal threats. Sleep eluded him that night, and in the grip of cold and fear, he pondered his predicament. He realised he had been immersed in fulfilling his duties per his master's advice and inadvertently overlooked the evolving environment. Despite faithfully procuring firewood and adapting his budget, he failed to recognise the changing circumstances that led to the market's depletion of dry trees. Now, finding himself without firewood one fateful night, cold and anxious, the realisation dawned that his lack of awareness had hindered his ability to respond to changes effectively. This revelation unfolded before him like magic, the profound hidden meaning of his master's wisdom, 'awareness'.

In the echo of that single word, the disciple gradually unravelled the profound teaching embedded within it. The monk was not merely referring to a passive state of being. He was imparting the art of mindful presence, an acute attentiveness to the surroundings and a deep understanding of the interconnectedness between oneself and one's responsibilities. **One cannot prepare for all possibilities and eventualities but must be aware to respond accordingly.**

Through the repetitive guidance of 'awareness', the disciple learned to observe, adapt and respond to the needs of the sanctuary by navigating challenges with a mindful heart and an awakened spirit.

Concluding this chapter and the entire book, I leave you with this profound story to serve as a guiding light.

Just as the monk entrusted his disciple with the sanctuary, businesses entrust professionals within the organisation to protect their organisational sanctuaries. Hence, here too, akin to the disciple's journey, success lies in the cultivation of 'awareness'. The profound simplicity of awareness becomes a guiding principle, empowering those professionals to observe, comprehend, adapt and ultimately protect sanctity.

Awareness is not merely about passive observation. It involves a keen understanding of organisational intricacies, potential risks and the dynamic interplay of various elements. A business analyst with heightened awareness is equipped to navigate challenges, adapt strategies and respond effectively to the ever-evolving business environment. Business analysts, equipped with a cyber security-oriented awareness and the support of security teams, become a proactive force in identifying potential risks. This involves not only understanding the dynamic nature of business requirements but also recognising the evolving landscape of cyber security threats. By comprehending the interconnectedness of these two aspects, a business analyst professional can contribute to creating resilient systems that can withstand the challenges posed by an ever-evolving digital environment.

Security is not a fixed destination but an ongoing journey, constantly adapting to the evolving landscape of threats and challenges. In the ever-changing horizon of business analysis and cyber security, the notion of security as a continuous journey emphasises the need for perpetual vigilance, adaptation and improvement. Organisations must remain proactive, anticipating potential risks and evolving their strategies in response.

The Business Analysis and Cyber Security Framework acknowledges this dynamic nature, providing a roadmap for professionals to navigate this continuous journey effectively. It encourages a mindset that embraces change, learning and adaptation, ensuring that security measures stay resilient in the face of emerging threats. As the digital landscape evolves, the framework guides professionals in maintaining a state of readiness, understanding that security is an ongoing process rather than a fixed endpoint.

This narrative, woven with the collective wisdom of business analysis and cyber security knowledge, the Business Analysis and Cyber Security Framework, content, stories, analogies and anecdotes, forms a holistic guide for your professional journey and within the organisational landscape. Let the amalgamation of the elements from these pages be your compass. May they steer and empower you to shape secure, resilient and robust systems within and beyond the boundaries of your professional pursuits.

REFLECTION TIME

Take a moment, ponder and write down:

- How do ethical considerations influence your approach to business analysis and cyber security? What changes would you make based on this influence?

TAKEAWAY QUESTIONS

- What are your key learning points in this chapter?
- What is the one lesson that you'll implement?
- What is your biggest takeaway from this book that might stay with you long into the future?

REFERENCES

CHAPTER 1

Barton, B. (1927) *What Can a Man Believe?* Bobbs-Merrill Co, Indianapolis.

Gilbert, E. (2016) 'Hobby, job, career, vocation'. Facebook. https://www.facebook.com/GilbertLiz/photos/a.356148997800555/948792035202912/

Paul, D. and Cadle J. (2020) *Business Analysis*, 4th edn. BCS, Swindon.

CHAPTER 2

AAG (2024) 'The latest 2024 cyber crime statistics (updated April 2024): headline cyber crime statistics'. AAG. https://aag-it.com/the-latest-cyber-crime-statistics/

BBC (2007) 'UK's families put on fraud alert'. BBC Online News. https://news.bbc.co.uk/1/hi/uk_politics/7103566.stm

BBC (2015) 'TalkTalk hack "affected 157,000 customers"'. BBC Online News. https://www.bbc.co.uk/news/business-34743185

Lauver, M. (2022) '53% of hospital IoT devices have security vulnerabilities'. Cynerio Research Report. https://www.securitymagazine.com/articles/97065-53-of-hospital-iot-devices-have-security-vulnerabilities

McLean, M. (2024) '2023 must-know cyber attack statistics and trends'. Embroker. https://www.embroker.com/blog/cyber-attack-statistics/

Nguyen, T. (2023) '4 emerging technologies you need to know about'. Gartner. https://www.gartner.com/en/articles/4-emerging-technologies-you-need-to-know-about

Sinek, S. (2019) *The Infinite Game: How Great Businesses Achieve Long-Lasting Success*. Portfolio Penguin, New York.

Van Kuiken, S. (2022) 'Tech at the edge: trends reshaping the future of IT and business'. McKinsey Digital. https://www.mckinsey.com/capabilities/mckinsey-digital/our-insights/tech-at-the-edge-trends-reshaping-the-future-of-it-and-business

Zacharakos, A. (2023) 'Studies show ransomware has already caused patient deaths'. TechTarget Security. https://www.techtarget.com/searchsecurity/feature/Studies-show-ransomware-has-already-caused-patient-deaths#:~:text=There%20have%20already%20been%20notable,lawsuit%20filed%20against%20the%20hospital

CHAPTER 3

CISCO (2024) 'What is cybersecurity?' CISCO Global. https://www.cisco.com/c/en_uk/products/security/what-is-cybersecurity.html

Dawkins, J. (2022) 'What's in a name? The origin of cyber'. CISO Global. https://www.ciso.inc/blog-posts/origin-cyber/#:~:text=Cyber%20Can%20be%20Traced%20Back%20to%20the%2040s&text=Cybernetics%20influences%20game%2C%20system%2C%20and,governance%E2%80%9D%20and%20applies%20to%20leadership

Eranti, V. and Lonkila, M. (2015) 'The social significance of the Facebook Like button'. *First Monday* 20 (6). https://doi.org/10.5210/fm.v20i6.5505.

Laughlin, A. (2021) 'How a smart home could be at risk from hackers'. Which? https://www.which.co.uk/news/article/how-the-smart-home-could-be-at-risk-from-hackers-akeR18s9eBHU

Singh, A.N. and Gupta, M.P. (2017) 'Information security management practices: case studies from India'. *Global Business Review* 20 (1), 253–271. https://doi.org/10.1177/0972150917721836.

Von Solms, B. (2000) 'Information security: the third wave?' *Computers and Security*, 19 (7), 615–620.

Von Solms, B. (2001) 'Information security: a multidimensional discipline'. *Computers and Security*, 20 (6), 504–508.

CHAPTER 4

Aufreiter, N., Huber, C. and Usher, O. (2022) 'The role of the board in preparing for extraordinary risk'. Inside the Strategy Room podcast, McKinsey & Company. https://www.mckinsey.com/capabilities/strategy-and-corporate-finance/our-insights/the-role-of-the-board-in-preparing-for-extraordinary-risk

Griffiths, C. (2024) 'The latest cloud computing statistics (updated April 2024)'. AAG. https://aag-it.com/the-latest-cloud-computing-statistics/

Nauck, F., Usher, O. and Weiss, L. (2020) 'The disaster you could have stopped: preparing for extraordinary risks'. McKinsey & Company. https://www.mckinsey.com/capabilities/risk-and-resilience/our-insights/the-disaster-you-could-have-stopped-preparing-for-extraordinary-risks

Sutton, D. (2021) *Information Risk Management: A Practitioner's Guide*. BCS, Swindon.

Vasudevan, M. (2016) *Mastering Leadership the Mousetrap Way: The Proven Path That Makes You the Leader Others Will Admire and Follow*. As Many Minds, Singapore.

Watkins, M.D. and Bazerman, M.H. (2003) 'Predictable surprises: the disasters you should have seen coming'. *Harvard Business Review*, April. https://hbr.org/2003/04/predictable-surprises-the-disasters-you-should-have-seen-coming

CHAPTER 5

IIBA (2015) *Business Analysis Body of Knowledge*. IIBA, Toronto, Canada.

IIBA (n.d.) 'A guide to the business analysis body of knowledge®' (BABOK® Guide). IIBA. https://www.iiba.org/career-resources/a-business-analysis-professionals-foundation-for-success/babok/

IIBA (n.d.) 'The business analysis core concept model™'. IIBA. https://www.iiba.org/knowledgehub/business-analysis-body-of-knowledge-babok-guide/2-business-analysis-key-concepts/2-1-the-business-analysis-core-concept-model/ (subscription required).

IIBA (n.d.) 'The BACCM checklist: 1.1.2'. IIBA. https://www.iiba.org/contentassets/24ef3 7ca6ae44cab972e50561f6c2721/1.1.2-baccm-checklist.pdf

CHAPTER 6

Cadle, J., Paul, D., Hunsley, J., Reed, A., Beckham, D. and Turner, P. (2021) *Business Analysis Techniques*, 3rd edn. BCS, Swindon.

Paul, D. and Cadle J. (2020) *Business Analysis*, 4th edn. BCS, Swindon.

Sondhi, R. (2008) *Total Strategy*, 3rd edn. BMC Global Services Publications, London.

CHAPTER 7

Daisyme, P. (2023) 'Data is the new currency. Don't let it slip through your fingers'. Due. https://due.com/data-new-currency/

McDonald, S. (2016) 'Ebola: a Big Data disaster'. The Centre for Internet and Society. https://cis-india.org/papers/ebola-a-big-data-disaster

Nunwick, A. (2023) 'Data to become new currency in the age of AI, says analyst'. Verdict. https://www.verdict.co.uk/data-to-become-new-currency-in-the-age-of-ai-says-analyst/?cf-view

Telford, S. and Verhulst, S.G. (2016) 'A framework for understanding data risk'. UR. https://understandrisk.org/a-framework-for-understanding-data-risk/

Thoughtspot (2023) 'The data chief: reimagining the banking experience with CDO of Singapore's GXS Bank'. Apple Podcasts. https://podcasts.apple.com/gb/podcast/reimagining-the-banking-experience-with-cdo-of/id1509495585?i=1000626167283

Zinieris, M. (n.d.) 'Data: a small four-letter word which has grown exponentially to such a big value'. Deloitte. https://www2.deloitte.com/cy/en/pages/technology/articles/data-grown-big-value.html

CHAPTER 8

BBC (2021) 'Russian pleads guilty to Tesla ransomware plot'. BBC Online News. https://www.bbc.co.uk/news/world-us-canada-56469475

Cadle, J., Paul, D., Hunsley, J., Reed, A., Beckham, D. and Turner, P. (2021) *Business Analysis Techniques*, 3rd edn. BCS, Swindon.

Gilmer, M. (n.d.) 'Bamboo is a determined plant'. The Ledger. https://eu.theledger.com/story/news/2009/12/19/bamboo-is-determined-plant/8033356007/

Seals, T. (2015) 'Social experiment highlights abysmal security hygiene'. *Infosecurity Magazine*, 20 October. https://www.infosecurity-magazine.com/news/social-experiment-abysmal-security/

Sergeyev, A. (2021) '3 powerful life lessons from the Chinese bamboo'. Timewiser.com. https://timewiser.com/blog/powerful-life-lessons-chinese-bamboo-story/

CHAPTER 9

Desruisseaux, D. (2017) 'The cyber security business case: an arduous challenge – part 1'. Schneider Electric Blog. https://blog.se.com/digital-transformation/cybersecurity/2017/05/05/cybersecurity-business-case-arduous-challenge-part-1/

Hyatt, C. (2020) 'The business case: how to construct a compelling argument for security initiatives, part 4'. Risk3sixty. https://risk3sixty.com/blog/how-to-build-a-business-case-for-security-initiatives-part-4

CHAPTER 10

Dittrich, D. and Kenneally, E. (eds) (2011) 'The Menlo report: ethical principles guiding information and communication technology research'. US Department of Homeland Security. www.dhs.gov/sites/default/files/publications/CSD-MenloPrinciplesCORE-20120803_1.pdf

Fox, J. (2018) 'An unlikeable truth: social media like buttons are designed to be addictive. They're impacting our ability to think rationally'. *Index on Censorship*, 47 (3), 11–13. https://doi.org/10.1177/0306422018800245.

Kumra, R. (2020) 'Tech ethics: avoiding unintended consequences'. LinkedIn Learning Courses. https://www.linkedin.com/learning/tech-ethics-avoiding-unintended-consequences/technology-and-consequences

Loi, M. and Christen, M. (2020) 'Ethical Frameworks for Cybersecurity'. In Christen, M., Gordijn, C. and Loi B. (eds), *The Ethics of Cybersecurity*. The International Library of Ethics, Law and Technology, vol 21. Springer, Cham. https://doi.org/10.1007/978-3-030-29053-5_4.

Nolan, C. (2023) *Oppenheimer*, Universal Pictures.

Philipson, A. (2024) *Einstein and the Bomb*, BBC Studios.

INDEX

Page numbers in italics refer to figures or tables.

organisational perception 103

outcomes *2, 3,* 46–7, 70, 86, 99, 103, 105, 119, 120

    business 73, 98, 101, 102

overconfidence 47

Parkerian Hexad 26, 27, *27*

Paul, Debra 1, 51, 66, 70

personally identifiable information (PII) 24, 27

personas 87–90

    bring-your-own-device (BYOD) user 88

    busy executive 88

    cautious user 87

    cyber extortionist 89

    cyber mercenary 89

    dark web user 89

    external hacker 89

    forgetful employee 88

    hacktivist 89

    insider threat 89

    malicious intent 89

    nation-state actor 89

    remote worker 88

    script kiddie 89

    social sharer 88

    tech-savvy professional 88

    unaware user 88

    uninformed executive 88

    unintentional insider threat 88

personnel security 28

PEST (political, economic, social, technological) analysis 67

PESTLE (political, economic, social, technological, legal, environmental) analysis 41, 51, 67–8, 94

phishing attacks 30

policy components 106–9

Porter's Five Forces model 51, 67

positive security approach 25, 26

possession 21, 27, 112

pre-emptive thinking 39

preparedness 92, 95–6, 116, 121

preventative security approach 25

principle of least privilege 80, 107

privacy impact assessment (PIA) 80

problem solvers 4

problem-solving skills 92, 105

process controls 24

protection of value 21, 22

ransom attacks 17

ransomware 17, 31, 85, 89

recovery strategies 78, 94, 115

reflections 7, 8, 11, 23, 37, 38, 47, 81, 91, 96, 105, 125

reliability 28, 71, 77

remote worker (personas) 88

requirements analysis 57–8, 73

requirements life cycle management 55–6

resilience 57, 68–70, 91, 101, 103, 122–3

    business 45, 82, 93, 96

    cyber 35, 44, 48, 99

risk 22

    acceptance 42

    analysis *24,* 35, 41, 79

    analysis (two pillars) 35, *36,* 50, 75, 113

    assessment 41, 55, 57, 67, 80, 83, 94, 100–1, 104, 109

    -averse 47

    avoidance 42

    bias 39, 46–7

    business analysis support 40–4, 46

    categories 121, 122

    communication and consultation 43

    conscious 35–9

    cyber security 36, 53, 55, 57, 62, 67, 80, 86–8, 90, 91

    data 44, 82, 115

    emerging 48, 121

    ethics of 119

    evaluation *40,* 41, *42,* 47

    existential 45, 93, 113

    framework 43, 44, 82, 115

    Global Risk Report (2020) 12

    high-impact 41, 45, 56

    identification 39–41, 47, 101

    information security 41

    management 29, 35, 36, 46, 91, 100, 101, 113

    management (AI) 48, 49

    management barriers 47

    management process 39–44, *40,* 48, 49, 103

    monitoring 44, 104

    perspectives 45–6

reduction 42, 101

    security 29, 41, 53, 55, 57–8, 62, 67, 73, 86–8, 90–1

    sharing 42

    treatment 41–4, 67

    unconscious 35–9, 48

robotic process automation (RPA) 48

role-based access 24, 25, 80

roles and responsibilities *7*

Rybak, Natasha 81, 82

scenario planning 93

script kiddie 89

security

    12 dimensions of information security 28–9

    approaches *25,* 34

    awareness 68, 71, 72, 80, 86, 107, 109

    definition 21, 22

    frameworks 13, 23

    goals 21, 26–8, 32, 57, 69

    initiatives 86, 100, 101, 102, 103, 105

    issues 74

    metrics 29, 54

    mindset 22–4, 30, 33, 35–6, 50, 64, 74–5, 79, *87, 98,* 112, 114–15, *117*

    objectives 21, 24–6, 29, 53–7, 59, 62, 69, 74

    organisation 28, 68

    personnel 28, 100

    physical and environmental 28

    policy 24–9, 98, 99, 106–10, 116

    policy and strategy 28

    projects 24, 104

    requirements 6, 10, 18, 24, 54–8, 67, 72–3, 79–80, 89, 108, 112

    risks 29, 41, 53, 55, 57–8, 62, 67, 73, 86–8, 90–1

    standards 13, 23, 27, 54, 116

    strategy 26–7, 68–9, 83, 87–8, 96, 104, 109, 115, 122

    violations 21, 26, 30

    vulnerabilities 64, 71–2, 74, 77, 80, 91

SharePoint 92

shifting left 64, 74, 114

Sinek, Simon 16, 112